ENDORSEMENTS

"With everyone talking about deconstruction these days, one might be hesitant to read yet another book on the topic. But Eric Scot English's *UN-enlightenment* isn't just another book. Rather than falling into one of two camps—as either an apologist for the status quo or one who wants to burn the whole faith to the ground—English finds a third way. He understands where Christianity has been, where it has gone wrong, and how it can move forward. And while you may not necessarily affirm every idea put forth in the book – that's not the intention of Progressive Christianity anyway—English gives his readers a lot of meat to chew on."

— **Matthew J. Distefano**, author of multiple books, co-host of the Heretic Happy Hour podcast, and columnist for Patheos

"What happens when you "say the sinner's prayer" and become an Evangelical in your teens, then go to an Evangelical college and seminary, but are never fully satisfied with the Evangelical framework you inherited? *UNenlightenment* reflects Eric English's experience of rethinking Evangelical theology. If you're a thoughtful person questioning elements of your belief system, you'll find real enlightenment in *UNenlightenment*."

— **Brian D. McLaren**, author of *Do I Stay Christian?*

"When someone like Eric English takes our mandate to seek God with all our heart, soul and mind as seriously as this, what you end up with is a book as deep and insightful as *UNenlightenment*. Prepare to be challenged, provoked and inspired by this exceptional work."

— **Keith Giles**, author of the 7-part *Jesus Un* series and *Sola Mysterium: Celebrating the Beautiful Uncertainty of Everything*

UN
ENLIGHTENMENT

A Theological Foundation for
Deconstructing and Reconstructing
the Christian Faith

ERIC SCOT ENGLISH

Copyright © 2022 by Eric English

Cover Design by Rafael Polendo (polendo.net)
Cover image by Bushko Oleksandr (Shutterstock.com)
Interior Layout by Matthew J. Distefano

Scriptures taken from the Holy Bible, New International Version®, NIV®. Copyright © 1973, 1978, 1984, 2011 by Biblica, Inc.™ Used by permission of Zondervan. All rights reserved worldwide. www.zondervan.com The "NIV" and "New International Version" are trademarks registered in the United States Patent and Trademark Office by Biblica, Inc.™

ISBN: 978-1-957007-30-4

This volume is printed on acid free paper and meets ANSI Z39.48 standards. Printed in the United States of America

Published by Quoir
Oak Glen, California
www.quoir.com

CONTENTS

ACKNOWLEDGMENTS

FIRST AND FOREMOST, I need to thank my wife, Cynthia, for her years of dedication to my work. From editing papers back in college to editing this book, she is my biggest fan, and I am hers. She forces me to be the greatest possible version of myself.

A special thanks to Anika Ojeda who took the time to not only read but dissect my manuscript to death. Her insights and arguments made a good book great.

A special thanks to my mother who used her much-needed resources to help me purchase books while in graduate school. Many of those books were used as research material for this book. I love you, Mom!

Thanks to Keith Giles for being a kind ear and always answering my questions about publishing.

Thanks to Rod Tucker for mentoring me through the publishing process and giving practical advice that helped me secure a publisher.

I also want to thank everyone who provided feedback and supported me through this process. You are too numerous to name, but you know who you are.

PREFACE

Twenty years ago, I began my journey to pursue an academic life. I was already a contemplative thinker, but I wanted to expand my knowledge. I wanted to write and teach. I wanted to live the life of a philosopher and share my unique perspective of the world with anyone who would listen.

However, as I attended various seminaries, I learned that many of these schools are not places of critical thinking. Instead, they are places where indoctrination is passed down from one generation to another. As a result, I was very unsatisfied with most of my graduate education.

I worked menial jobs during much of my graduate education, which allowed me to write. I wrote with any free moment I had—lunch breaks, in-between customers, etc. I wrote in journals, on little scraps of paper, whatever I could find to write an idea down.

Fast forward 20 years and I still have all those little scraps of papers and journal entries—and I've added to them over the years. All of those scraps of papers were attempts to solve problems, problems in philosophy, theology, contemporary culture, the Church, etc. Looking back, I realize that what I was really doing was deconstructing my Christian faith. I identified problems that I found within the Church and its beliefs and tried to solve those issues on my little scraps of paper.

What you hold in your hand are those little scraps of paper, those journal pages, and backs of napkins. Many of those ideas are contained here in this book. This book represents my deconstruction and reconstruction journey. It's a journey I share with you in hopes that it will help you in your own journey.

Important Disclaimers

I have grown weary of evangelicals misrepresenting what progressive Christians believe. This book is, in part, a response to this misrepresentation. I want to set the record straight about what progressive Christianity is and is not—both for the detractors, but also for the weary Christian travelers who find themselves on the road of deconstruction. Contained within these pages are not only my thoughts, but also the thoughts of some of the leading progressive thinkers around the world—as well as throughout history.

It is important to underscore the wide-ranging beliefs that progressive Christians have. A single book cannot represent all the diverse beliefs held by the individuals in this diverse group. Additionally, not all traditional theological loci have been thoroughly considered, but only those that seem the most important. In these cases, I put forth a cogent articulation of what I believe to be a progressive perspective.

It is also the case that not every theological topic presented in this book will stray from its conservative, evangelical/orthodox origin. In these cases, I either put forth the orthodox perspective, or I omit discussion of it entirely.

There is another tangential reason for writing this book—to challenge the establishment. Most theology is a product of the academy and, therefore, is oftentimes written within a particular denominational context. For this reason, most theologians are unable to explore their thinking beyond their denominational parameters. I, on the other hand, am not bound by any parameters except those of my own convictions. I can bring an unfettered perspective as a result.

You will notice that divine pronouns are not capitalized in this book. This is purposeful, to demonstrate the nature of God does not comprise any specific gender (e.g., He). God is above and beyond our gender norms and should, therefore, be reflected in some way within our language. To capitalize these pronouns is to add extra emphasis to a fact that I do not believe exists. With that said, I have kept the gendered pronouns themselves limited where it aids readability.

Lastly, it's important to address my use of the term "evangelical." I use this term because the majority of progressive Christians come out of evangelicalism. My critiques are NOT against "evangelicals" per se, but against "evangelicalism." My arguments are against the institution, which perpetuates a dogma that continues to ostracize and persecute. This institution consists of academics who continue to teach their budding pastors false doctrines, which then trickles down to laypeople. I hope that critically thinking evangelicals will view these pages openly and in such a way that they re-evaluate the institutions their beliefs are associated with.

INTRODUCTION

THEOLOGY IS THE STUDY of God. Theology should be beautiful, poetic, relevant, and memorable. It should create a desire within the individual to learn more about God. However, most theology books that exist are stuffy—loaded with academic language that is intended for other academics. Very rarely is a theology book written for the common intellectual. Very rarely does a theology book motivate a person to live differently.

This book is not meant to be a definitive work of theology about progressive Christianity. No such book could or should ever be written. Instead, the purpose of this book is two-fold. First, it can serve as an introduction for those who desire to know more about progressive Christianity and why it holds certain theological beliefs. Second, this book is meant to provide a framework for those within progressive Christianity to better formulate and articulate their own reconstructionist theology.

In order to discuss a progressive theology, it is first important to understand what is meant by "progressive." The term progressive is not a political affiliation,[1] but rather a cultural-theological one. The term "progressive" for better or worse is used to differentiate itself from conservative *and* liberal theological thinking. Oftentimes, the term "progressive" is used synonymously with "dynamic." Since culture is always in dynamic flux, progressive theology is flexible enough to manage changes within the everchanging cultural milieu—something liberal and conservative Christianity is oftentimes unable to accomplish.

A Brief History of Progressive Christianity

There is not currently a book that traces the heritage of progressive Christianity. This is partly because progressive Christianity is not that old, but the other reason is that it has varied in form throughout its history. One of the things I attempt to do in this book is to trace progressive Christianity back to the original source. This is not meant to be comprehensive, but a brief survey for contextual purposes.

Much of progressive Christianity comes out of various evangelical movements, such as Christian Postmodernism, the Emerging Church, and the missional church movement. This history – although present in the latter part of the 1980s under the generic guise of postmodern Christianity - didn't really become organized until the late 1990s and early 2000s. The progressive movement was a product of two major phenomena: First, youth pastors who were trying to figure out how to minister to a new generation of Christians, and secondly, postmodern evangelical church planting. Collectively, these churches became known as "emerging" churches; that is, churches that were emerging from out of evangelicalism.[2]

Individuals like Tony Jones, Brian McLaren, and Doug Pagitt were the main voices of the emergent movement during this time. As such, they were also the target of much criticism by evangelicals who consistently labeled them "postmodern."[3] As a result of their work, small churches sprang up throughout the country—many of which simply met in homes. The emphasis of these early "emerging" churches was to remain small so that they could stay connected to the community in which they ministered. With the explosion of these emerging churches from the early 2000s onward, there were many variations of emergence that would later go under the generic title of progressive Christianity.

There has been a sharp decline in the percentage of people identifying as "evangelical" in the U.S. from the late 2000s to the time of this writing

(2022). This trend can be linked to an increase in those who call themselves "progressive."[4] Much of this can be attributed to those within evangelicalism going through "deconstruction." Deconstruction and the new faith that emerges (or the lack of faith that emerges) are arguably the most significant influences for individuals leaving evangelicalism. The data shows that those who deconstruct typically leave the church entirely or begin attending a non-evangelical church.[5]

Many people who find themselves in progressive Christianity are there because they have deconstructed from their conservative, evangelical faith. As a result, progressive Christianity boasts a wide range of beliefs about various theological doctrines. I see my task here as not to dictate what people are to believe, but rather to try and find the theological center where theologies overlap within progressive Christianity.

If there are any core axioms to those who call themselves "progressive," then it might be that there is no distinction between belief and behavior. Oftentimes in evangelical theology, belief is a separate intellectual task, which may or may not be followed by some accompanying behavior. However, in progressive theology, much of the truth of a proposition is not wrapped up in the content, but in the accompanying behavior. Over the years this has been referred to as a speech-act, which we will discuss in greater detail in forthcoming chapters.[6]

My Time in Evangelicalism

I spent the first 15 years of my Christian life steeped in evangelicalism. I was 16 when I became a Christian. My experience with "getting saved" or becoming "born again" was not that uncommon. I had dinner with an "evangelist" from the local Baptist church and he brought me through the "Romans Road" using a tract. The tract had all the usual fundamentalist stuff: people on fire, a cross bridging a gap which leads to Heaven, stuff about how terrible of a human being I was, etc. Luckily, I was already severely depressed, so I felt like a terrible person anyway. I accepted Jesus as my "savior" that night because I thought he would help me feel better and I could develop better friendships.

The Baptist church I attended went through a major split within a year of my conversion. Apparently, some in the church thought that it was inappropriate for the pastor's daughter to attend prom. The pastor then had a heart attack over the stress of it and was rushed to the ER one night. Immediately, I saw the ugly side of church politics and evangelicalism.

Shortly thereafter, I attended college at a local evangelical institution that prided itself in exploring the biblical narrative and the arts to help students develop a "biblical worldview." I devoured my Bible and theology classes. I loved hearing about missions and the importance of being socially aware. I participated in several ministries and spoke at various outreach events. I thrived in this environment where I felt freer to express my religious beliefs than I had in high school.

During my second year of college, I found myself without a place to live. I set up a meeting with the associate pastor of the megachurch where I volunteered. In the meeting, I asked whether he could help me find a place to live for a couple of months. The answer was a resounding, "No." He went on to explain, "We have already asked a lot of our congregation to help us build a new building. We cannot burden them with something like this." I was both distraught and confused as to why a church would respond in this way. Eventually, after several weeks of living out of my car, I stayed with a friend and her family until a more permanent solution was found.

Thankfully, college wasn't all church politics and homelessness. I also met my future wife there. During our engagement, we did premarital counseling with our evangelical pastor, who one day informed us that he could not in good conscience endorse our marriage. The reason he gave was that he did not think I would make a good "provider" for my wife. Believe it or not, his words were prophetic. My wife is a great provider and good for her! I could not be prouder of what she has achieved. We left the evangelical church we attended not long after that pre-martial session – an environment where my wife would have certainly been discouraged from such ambitions.

I attended seminary shortly after finishing college. It was there that I first realized that the social justice outreach that I was taught in college was a ruse. I began encountering thinkers like Brian McLaren and Tony Jones who were calling the Church to be more socially aware. At the same time my seminary professors were criticizing the same thinkers for being heretics. It did not make any sense to me because I was always under the impression that the Church was supposed to care about things like poverty and helping the disenfranchised. I have since come to realize the reason had nothing to do with theology and had everything to do with politics. People like McLaren and Jones sounded way too much like liberals and, therefore, assumptions were made about their theological positions as a result.

I could fill a book with stories like these from my years in evangelicalism. I have listened to the experiences of my brothers and sisters who echo the same stories - stories of being ostracized, rejected, and fired from ministry positions over theo-political issues. Over the last two decades, I watched as evangelicalism slowly abandoned its calling to love its neighbor in favor of political power and influence. A larger inventory of the situation later revealed to me that evangelicalism as an organization was always political, and their love of neighbor was, in many ways, a means for bolstering political power. Of course, this is not universal among the people who make up evangelicalism but is predominant among organizing bodies of evangelicals. To reiterate, much of my argument is not against the people who make up evangelicalism because they are simply pawns in a larger political agenda. (To be sure, I had positive experiences while among them as well.)

These experiences led me to deconstruct and reconstruct my faith over the last 25 years. It has been a difficult journey, but I am tethered by two important things: First, I never lost my desire to be a critical thinker. Anyone can be a critical thinker. It simply takes desire. Second, I have always been committed to reading and interacting with people and ideas different from my own. I strongly believe that no one perspective has it all right. It's oftentimes the little bits from multiple perspectives that lead a person to the truth.

Defining Evangelicalism

It is important to define my use of the term evangelical. The National Association of Evangelicals has a definition that is taken from the historian David Bebbington. It states that evangelicals can be identified by the following characteristics:

- **Conversionism**: the belief that lives need to be transformed through a "born-again" experience and a lifelong process of following Jesus

- **Activism**: the expression and demonstration of the Gospel in missionary and social reform efforts

- **Biblicism**: a high regard for and obedience to the Bible as the ultimate authority

- **Crucicentrism**: a stress on the sacrifice of Jesus Christ on the cross as making possible the redemption of humanity.

Although these principles are used to define evangelicals, they are largely unhelpful on their own. Many non-evangelicals can fall into the same beliefs. Therefore, I will add to this list the following principles:

- **Conversionism**: Jesus is the only way to God.

- **Activism**: No additions

- **Biblicism**: The Bible is the inerrant Word of God.

- **Crucicentrism**: Jesus Christ is the only atoning sacrifice for the forgiveness of sins.

There are also variations within evangelicalism, such as mainstream and liberal evangelicalism. I do not differentiate between those subgroups for the purposes of this book. Instead, I have defined evangelical using the aforementioned criteria regardless of one's subgrouping within it.

How to Use This Book

I wrote this book so that it could be used in a couple of different ways. First and foremost, it is a foundation for those who are going through the deconstruction and reconstruction phases of their faith journey. This book deconstructs certain aspects of the Christian faith and then reconstructs it in a progressive theological framework. I should note that not all doctrines presented are new reconstructions. In some cases, reconstruction should and does reaffirm some classical orthodox ideas. This should be the case because not all theological beliefs from any given denomination or religious institution are faulty.

Secondly, this can be read as a book of progressive theology. Like any theology that claims to represent a perspective, there will be some who disagree with the premise that this represents progressive theology in its fullest expression. To those, I would say that I agree. This book is not intended to be all-inclusive, but instead a foundation from which to build upon. With any book of theology, there will be those within the tradition that disagree. That is okay. I hope that this at least captures the "progressive spirit" and can provoke conversations moving forward.

The Structure of the Book

Most of the chapters have the same organizational structure. Each chapter begins with an introduction to the main idea. It asks important, relevant questions that are necessary for the reader to consider. In most cases, there is an evangelical or "traditional" perspective that is explained and then deconstructed. From there I go through the steps of reconstructing the idea from a progressive perspective in order to demonstrate how one can answer the important questions related to the idea under discussion.

The first chapter of this book, "UNenlightenment," discloses my presuppositions and why I think they are an important context for moving forward to the chapters that follow. Next, I discuss methodology and revelation. I include the philosophical issue of truth since one's perspective on truth is paramount to how one approaches reading Scripture.

Later in the book, I deal with the traditional theological loci of the Trinity: the father, the son, and the Spirit. Next, I deal with creation and humanity in order to help us better understand the world around us and how we are connected to that creation. From there, I deal with the cultural and social issues that often divide progressives and evangelicals in the section entitled, "the Church, Culture and the Christian life." Finally, I included a "Postscript" to encourage those going through the process of deconstruction and to provide some rudimentary psychological advice to help them get through this difficult, yet exciting, period in their lives.

Since many of my criticisms in this book have to do with evangelical hermeneutics, I also included an appendix called, "Narrative Perspectivism: An Introduction" that discusses a new way to view hermeneutics.

I also included one of my articles in Appendix B which was published almost 10 years ago. This article went viral for Patheos.com and was an important first step in setting my trajectory leading to this book.

Finally, Appendix C is a list of resources that those going through this process can rely on to help in their journey.

"Very truly I tell you, no one can see the kingdom of God unless they are born again."

— John 3:3 (NIV)

1

UNENLIGHTENMENT

"Christendom has often achieved apparent success by ignoring the precepts of its founder."
—H. Richard Niebuhr

"Doubt is not the opposite of faith; it is one element of faith."
—Paul Tillich

I WRITE A COLUMN for Patheos.com called *UNenlightenment* and host a podcast by the same name. The question I get asked most is, "what does UNenlightenment mean?" It's a difficult question to answer in a sound bite, so I am thankful to be able to dedicate a chapter to unravel this idea. After all, UNenlightenment is the crucial first step in faith deconstruction.

UNenlightenment is the unlearning of Enlightenment presuppositions, which often prevent Christians from understanding the truth of the Gospel. Nearly everything within Modern Christianity has been influenced by the

Enlightenment—from the way we do church to the theology we teach our pastors and the behaviors of Christians in the culture at large.[1] UNenlightenment is the process of unlearning our harmful beliefs (deconstruction), then re-understanding Scripture and faith (reconstruction), and finally, using that information to live the Gospel anew in the world.

More specifically, UNenlightenment is about deconstructing the historical and theological narratives we've inherited. This deconstruction journey is difficult but necessary. Deconstruction helps us to see clearly enough to start to put this convoluted puzzle of Christianity back together again. Progressive Christianity provides a home for weary travelers as they unravel traditional narratives and reconstruct them into something coherent.

How We Got Here: A Very Brief History

From the time of Constantine (311 CE) through the Middle Ages (1520 CE), the Christian Church was the primary power broker of knowledge in the Western world. The scientific revolution called into question something the Church had believed its entire history; namely, that God created *ex nihilo* (from nothing) everything within the universe and, as such, placed humanity at the center of this created cosmos. However, scientific discovery theorized the falsehood of this belief. The scientific community also claimed the Earth was not at the center of the universe, which implied that humanity was not as important as many Christians believed. Furthermore, there was a great distrust that grew toward the Church—and rightfully so. It was during this period of hostility that French philosopher, Rene Descartes, entered the picture. He famously asserted that we have to begin anew by doubting everything that we have been taught. Descartes's belief that doubt was the chief constituent of knowledge ushered in a new period known as the Enlightenment. To be clear, Descartes's doubt as the chief constituent of knowledge was based upon his acknowledgment that doubt itself was the only aspect of knowledge that could not be doubted. This was known as *cogito, ergo sum* (I think, therefore, I am.) Descartes's plea to doubt everything stemmed from a skepticism that still reverberates today. The scientific revolution provided "answers" to questions only previously answered by the Church. As a result, the skepticism of the time was directed specifically toward the Church.

Building upon this single-direction skepticism, G.W.F. Hegel (the Forefather of Modernism; 1770-1831) sought to use dialectic to identify the source for absolute truth. Dialectic is a method for establishing true propositions. It consists of a thesis (or the thing being considered), antithesis (the main proposition's opposite), and synthesis (what is found in the middle of the thesis and its antithesis).

Up to this point, the Church had been largely silent in the larger philosophical conversation. It had a choice when it came to Hegel; it could adopt Hegelianism, or it could fight against it. Despite Soren Kierkegaard's warning to the Church—specifically the Lutheran State Church within Denmark—to reject Hegel's teachings, many within the Church adopted the Hegelian worldview.

It was a perfect marriage for the Church because they could use Hegelianism to proclaim the absolute truth of Scripture. What the Church could not foresee is that science also jumped on board and, as a result of Hegelianism, developed the scientific method. What once seemed like the perfect marriage was now in trouble as the scientific worldview would seemingly be the new power broker of knowledge on into the 20th century.

From the mid-19th century onward, Modernism became the conduit for the scientific method, evolution, industrialism, and the resurgence of atheism, among other things. In the early 20th century, the Church's response to the development of science as a power broker of knowledge was fundamentalism. Holding Modernism on one hand and God on the other, fundamentalists sought to discredit evolution and other scientific hypotheses by going "back to the Bible." It is during this time that doctrines like inerrancy became critical to providing the link between modern thinking and God. Inerrancy was the fundamentalist's way of skirting around Modernism's version of truth by asserting *a priori* (apart from evidence) that the Bible was without error.

Fundamentalism was largely unsuccessful. By the time World War II arrived, fundamentalism had moved on to different issues. Evangelicalism opposed the separatist nature of fundamentalism and desired to reconnect the Church to the culture. Primarily through people like Billy Graham, this reconnection was hugely successful. This was also a time of great economic growth in the United States. The added economic benefits helped to spur on huge church growth throughout the 1950s and 1960s. Evangelicalism continued to grow through the 1970s and 1980s.

It was during this growth that it moved in a different direction—toward politics. There were many people responsible for this. Individuals like Francis Schaeffer and his son Frank, who started and perpetuated the pro-life movement, James Dobson who began Focus on the Family, which is a public policy advocacy group, and Jerry Falwell Sr., who began the religious right movement. These are just a few of the many evangelicals who pushed evangelicalism into the political realm all under the banner of advancing the Kingdom.[2]

The transition to Postmodernism started during the 1970s. However, the Church largely stayed in Modernism—refusing to embrace the change necessary to stay connected to culture. The primary reason the Church—and specifically evangelicalism—did this is because it refused to trade in the objective certainty that Modernism granted them for the subjective uncertainty that accompanied Postmodernism.

Moreover, this is why so much of evangelicalism's cultural beliefs seem archaic and uninformed; the culture is viewed from an outdated worldview. What's more, evangelicals are taught by their leaders that what they hold is not an outdated modern worldview, but a "biblical worldview." This means that when culture supposedly opposes evangelicals, in essence, they are opposing the Christian worldview set forth by Scripture. However, this worldview was not set forth by Scripture, but rather by Modernism.

UNenlightenment thinking permits us to rewind the record of history, apart from the presuppositions that plague much of our understanding. It permits us to doubt again, as Descartes did. But we must not stop there unless we want to spiral out of control down a nihilistic rabbit hole. Instead, we must have the courage to pick ourselves back up and reconstruct a new set of beliefs (and perhaps re-establish some old ones.)

Unlike what many evangelicals are taught, science is not the enemy. Science allows humanity to progress. God uses science to illuminate our understanding of ourselves and the world around us. Therefore, we should not view science as something contradicting religion. Instead, we should look to harmonize the two so that we might better understand what God has given us.

Christianity's common enemy ought not to be science, but rather injustice. Christians must work out their faith – whatever that looks like, in such a way that they are united under this common purpose. They should seek out *reconciliation*. They should seek out ways to *love* and *care for others*. It is what Christ did by the way he lived his life, and it is what Christians are called to do every day. We'll discuss this concept more in the coming chapters.

The Problem of Evangelicalism and Apologetics

Evangelicalism is the chief Protestant product of the Enlightenment in the West. Evangelicalism has largely bought into the proposition that objectivity is the primary means of measurement for biblical truth. This is best illustrated through modern evangelical apologetics (the art of defending the faith), which adopts scientific principles for much of its methodology.[3] As a result, at the core of defending their faith is the full reliance upon scientific investigative principles and logic. Somehow, by using these scientific principles, evangelicalism can "prove" the existence of a metaphysical deity (or at least justify the existence of one). This may sound strange since it seems axiomatic that evangelicalism is anti-science. And yet, evangelical theologians use scientific principles all the time - from trying to understand history to biblical archeology to the creation of systematic theology itself.

Evangelical apologetics ultimately begins with the presumption of absolute truth. That is, humans can objectively know or understand certain things—like God. Just like any theory of knowledge, one must buy into the presuppositions that it asserts, even if those suppositions are incorrect. When it comes to absolutism, apologetics is assuming a Hegelian (and by extension Scientism's) view of truth.

This is not an evangelical problem, per se. It is a problem of Modernism. Modernistic thinking is so ingrained in our minds today that few question it. Modernistic thinking forces one to evaluate metaphysical truths using objective measurements—both science and evangelicalism influences people in this direction. The bottom line is that you cannot prove the existence of a metaphysical deity using a physical methodology.

One might even be able to make the case that modern apologetics is useless, at least in a formal sense, in today's world. It not only suffers from the aforementioned problems, but it also presupposes that there is some proposition that *needs* to be defended. Why are Christians required to be on the defensive just because they are religious? This is the assumption that apologetics makes before it has even begun its task.

Anyone has the right to believe in God and that belief is warranted on the sole basis that it is reasonable to do so.[4] Nobody has to defend this right and if some other wants to believe that God does not exist then they are also warranted to do so. Defensiveness, particularly aggressive and targeted defensiveness, seems to miss the point of the Gospel.

The best form of apologetics is one communicated not by words or memorized arguments, but in the lives that we live. The way one lives their life has no counterargument. Displaying the love of Jesus to others is the only argument that one needs; it is the only proof that is required. It is proof that the people of God serve something beyond themselves. Jesus agreed with this sentiment, as he is quoted in John 13:35 saying, "By this everyone will know that you are my disciples, if you love one another."

One of the primary principles of evangelicalism is their emphasis on evangelism - bringing others to Christ. It has been difficult for evangelicals to break through the impersonal Billy Graham style of "witnessing." However, Christians cannot give people the hope they have in Christ in a one-time conversation. Instead, there has to be a relationship that exists. There has to be trust – the type of trust that one establishes over a period of time. What's more, providing people with the hope of Christ may not even be a conversation, but an expression of what they see Christians do. Right now, what non-Christians see from many Christians is not that appealing.

Based upon the actions of many evangelicals in our culture, the good news is not really all that good. Oftentimes, conversion to Christianity is perceived by non-Christians as one becoming a bigoted, transphobic, hypocritical Republican. Evangelicals will argue that the reason for this perception is a growing secular culture that opposes religious values. However, according to a Pew Research Center survey conducted with U.S. adults in 2017,[5] Americans are expressing warmer feelings towards religious groups – particularly Jews and Catholics, with the exception being evangelicals. What many of us fail to realize is that there is transformative power in a life well-lived. People are tired of hearing about Jesus and how they are going to Hell. What they need is to start seeing him in the world through his followers. This must be the new way of evangelism.

The Theo-Political Problem of Evangelicalism

There is a truth about evangelicalism that is not easily observed by those within that worldview. Namely, there exists a lack of delineation between the Kingdom of God and the kingdom of man. This theo-political capitulation is obvious to those looking from the outside in, but not so obvious if you are viewing the world from within evangelicalism. What is clear is that evangelical leaders perpetuate the problem, which then gets distributed and rehashed throughout evangelicalism's echo chamber.

Here is a contemporary example of how this plays out in the real world. The Southern Baptist Convention (SBC) is the largest evangelical denomination in the United States. They routinely vote on measures for their denomination in lockstep with the Republican Party's policies. For example, in 2021, their agenda was primarily to determine a position on Critical Race Theory and whether to take further actions about claims of sexual abuse against leaders within the SBC. Since both topics were primarily liberal issues, they came out against both – arguing that CRT is not biblical and refusing to investigate any further the claims of sexual abuse against SBC leaders. It was only after several prominent SBC leaders left or threatened to leave the SBC over the rulings that SBC leadership decided to actually take a deeper look at the issues. This is one example of a political default that is oftentimes bolstered by fanatic leadership within evangelicalism.

There is also a lot of predatory behavior in evangelicalism, both sexual and spiritual. Despite this, many men within evangelicalism stay in power even when they have taken advantage of women and children. The same people who decried that the Catholic Church clean up their house are now being exposed as sexual and spiritual predators by the movements like #MeToo. People like Jerry Falwell Jr., Mark Driscoll, Bill Hybels, and Ravi Zacharias (just to name a few) have been able to stay in power for a time even though they are or have been abusive.

Everything Comes Together into Christendom

Christendom is the convergence of church and state into an indistinguishable entity. Evangelicalism finds itself in this theo-political drama due to an inherent motivation towards Christendom. That is, God will bless the nation that finds itself dedicated to believing in him. But there is a question one must ask regarding this: Is a nation "Christian" because of the number of people who claim to be such? Or is a nation Christian because its leaders use Christian values to govern the country? Or both?

Those who advocate for Christendom envisage a country that upholds biblical values both formally (legislatively) and informally (culturally). There are generally two types of proponents for Christendom. The first sees the U.S. as a country not that different from the nation of Israel in the Hebrew Scriptures. They would like to see the U.S. run like a Christian theocracy. An example of those belonging to this group are Christian nationalists - notably, most of whom are white.

The second group is less extreme, but equally dangerous – perhaps even more so. These individuals desire something more subversive whereby the government is used only as a means of upholding cultural values through legislative practices. For proponents of this version of Christendom, the U.S. doesn't have to be a formal theocracy only an informal one. Ultimate power is the chief aim. To people like this, the end justifies the means, which means that Christianity is used to disguise its real motivations.

Many people of this persuasion will argue that the Founding Fathers intended to create a Christian nation and that this can be observed in the language used throughout the U.S. Constitution and other tangential writings from these men. It's important to understand that when our country was founded, it was largely a "God-fearing" country. This is different from being a Christian nation. One does not have to be a Christian to be "God-fearing." Most people during the time of the American Revolution had a general respect for God and some of those people were Christian. The Founders of our country were no different. They reflected the context of the nation as a whole, which was a melting pot of various beliefs.

It was considered a formal courtesy to acknowledge God on official documents and formal correspondence during that time. This was a carry-over from the traditions of England. The acknowledgment of God on various constitutional papers and books was idiomatic. This was akin to a bailiff asking someone to place their hand on the Bible during a court proceeding and swearing to God that they will tell the truth. It's simply a formal way of asking, "Do you promise to tell the truth?"

Readers must understand the writings contextually when interpreting documents from a different time in history and resist the urge to superimpose their own perspective upon the text. When this is done with constitutional documents and tangential writings, it is clear that, although the Founding Fathers had respect for God (and some were Christians in their own right), they were not attempting to form a nation that was governed by Christian Scriptures.

Furthermore, there is no mention in our constitution of the formation of a Christian nation. Any reference to God in any official documentation is purposefully generic as many people believed in some sort of deity, including Jews and Muslims. Therefore, if one is basing their decision on whether the United States is a Christian nation on the mention of God in historical documents, then both Jews, Muslims, and any other religious group who worship a God have the same right to the claim.

The United States is, and always has been, a secular nation; a nation that was conceived to be a place of refuge for "the tired, the poor, and the huddled masses yearning to breathe free." The first immigrants, and many who followed, came to this land seeking religious freedom from the tyranny of religious statehood. It doesn't make sense that the Founding Fathers would create the same type of government that their constituents had a history of fleeing from.

A secular nation does not mean an anti-Christian nation, despite what evangelicals would have you believe. Instead, it means an impartial nation. Ironically, for Christians to remain free they must embrace the secularism that will impartially protect their religious freedom.

There does seem to be a correlation between how evangelicals interpret Scripture and how they understand history. In both cases, they often superimpose their idea of God onto the text. In the case of our nation's historical documents, they are taking the literal God of *their* belief and superimposing it over our Founding Fathers' idea of God.

The main reason why so many evangelicals have gone along with this charade is because of what Kierkegaard called the "problem of the crowd"[6] and what psychology calls "groupthink."[7] This idea states that when you have a group of individuals who maintain proximity to one another, they tend to think similarly. The individual begins to lose their identity for the sake of the group's identity. This happens mainly because an individual is willing to give up personal identity if they can associate themselves with an idea that has group support. When Christians take on specific identities that ultimately overshadow their primary identity as Christ-followers (such as denominational and even political identities), they can become theologically and philosophically confined to the group and lose who they are.

People often worry that departing from the thinking of a group will result in some form of ostracization. This is certainly true in many cases, but the more important question should be, "who is the group loyal to? Jesus, their denomination, or some political affiliation?" Few experience this expulsion more than progressive Christians, who through the act of questioning, are oftentimes ostracized.

In today's day and age, there is an ever-fading line between the kingdom of man and the Kingdom of God. The more people attempt to pursue a utopian society (based on their own particular beliefs and convictions), the farther they will be from the Kingdom of God. The establishment of the Kingdom of God is not a contingent future event. The Kingdom of God is already here. It is seen through how we welcome the refugee. It can be observed through the acts of feeding the hungry, housing the poor, caring for widows and orphans, and loving our neighbors *and* our enemies. The Kingdom is built on how we treat those who are often dubbed as "the least of these."[8]

The Problem of Systematic Theology

The majority of evangelical theology is systematic. Systematic theology is the systematic organization of theological propositions. These propositions are then arranged into various theological loci. It's primarily a 20th century phenomenon[9] and is the direct result of the capitulation evangelicalism has largely made to modernistic thinking.

One might wonder, "What is wrong with having an organized theology?" A little comment here will suffice for now as this topic is covered more fully in the next chapter. Systematic Theology is a result of propositionalism. Propositionalism is the belief that since the text of the Bible is objectively true, that one can extract various propositions from it to create meaning regardless of context. Systematic theology then organizes those propositions into theological loci as fodder for larger theological claims.

The problem with all of this is that the Bible is not scientific – it's not always logical and is, at times, messy. Taking a systematic approach to theology means that one is forced to render conclusions for the sake of the system, instead of for the sake of truth. What's more, when a system finds incongruities, the whole system is deemed untrue – which leads proponents to deny or attempt to justify what may look like an incongruity to reframe it as truth. Logic is the measure by which a system is considered plausible instead of what is true. It forces one to look at Scripture propositionally (like an encyclopedia of truth claims), instead of narratively.[10] I have included an alternative to systematic theology in Appendix A.

Systematic theology is what happens when you adhere to a scientific, modern methodology. Scientific systems require adherence to an objective methodology. There is nothing inherently wrong with objective methodologies. In many cases, they serve us well – we enjoy products every day because of strict adherence to scientific methodologies. However, it doesn't work when you are dealing with metaphysical ideas. Metaphysical ideas cannot be submitted to a physical, scientific methodology because metaphysical ideas are not tangible.

To make systematic theology work within a physical methodology, the method has to have a foundational rule that governs the whole enterprise – just like scientific methodologies do. That rule: *A conclusion is true only if it has correspondence to something in the real world.* For example, a granite rock can only be a granite rock if there are granite rocks in the world. We can point to the rock and confidently say, "that is a granite rock" because it is proven to comprise the right elements that make it a granite rock through empirical testing.

In an objective system, theology has to point to the real world for verification. Instead, evangelical theology points to the rule of inerrancy. Inerrancy allows the practitioner to reframe truth in light of itself, instead of what is. This has to be done because truth has to be compared to something for it to be known as such. Moreover, as long as the rules of inerrancy are followed, one can extrapolate "truth," even if ultimately, the proposition is not true. Here truth is not compared to reality because there is no way to compare something physical with something metaphysical. Instead, it only has to meet the conditions set by inerrancy for it to be true.

However, what if it is possible to verify what is in Scripture with the real world without the need for inerrancy? I believe we can do this, but it requires many of us to relinquish some long-held and cherished beliefs. Ultimately, this is the hope for a progressive theology.

The Hope for Progressive Theology

The hope for progressive theology is that it can provide a dynamic lens through which individuals can view God and Scripture. Oftentimes, when non-progressives hear "dynamic" they immediately infer that it refers to God's immutability or that he changes from generation to generation depending on cultural context. However, this is a completely disconnected perspective. Perhaps the best way to understand this dynamism within an immutable framework is to understand that the Gospel never changes, but our cultural perspectives do. Therefore, interpretive conclusions can change based on a change of perspective or the introduction of additional information that was not known previously.

The evangelical church's theology is static, which is why it takes so long for their churches to catch up with cultural evolutions. Oftentimes within evangelicalism, immutability overflows into their impressions of the culture, resulting in an absurdly slow evolution of change. Evangelicalism oftentimes finds itself being reactive to cultural phenomenon instead of being proactive and leading culture into the truth of God's love for his people.

Progressive Theology Does Not Mean Liberal Theology

Unlike liberal politics, the term "progressive" - as used in progressive Christianity - does not mean liberal or left of liberal. It's a catch-all phrase used to denote a group of Christians who have been or would be ostracized for their beliefs by conservative Christians. It also consists of people just tired of the evangelical way of doing things.

Progressive Christianity refers to a large group of people with a large swath of beliefs. Progressive Christianity is not a denomination within Christianity, but instead describes a type of Christian. Progressive Christians exist in many different denominational contexts. Many progressives can be found in mainline denominations, and some can even be found in evangelicalism. In other words, even though some churches may consider themselves "progressive," progressive Christianity is not denominational.

There is a temptation to pigeonhole progressive theology into liberalism by asserting that their primary cause is social justice. Although social responsibility is a hallmark of progressive theology, it in no way captures the essence of progressive theology like it does with liberal theology. Moreover, progressive theology should be understood as a reorientation that takes seriously the humanity of the Gospel – the humanity of Jesus. Progressive theology looks to demystify the metaphysical Jesus that is often found in evangelical churches for a Jesus that is much more like us; a Jesus that we can relate to; a Jesus that we can follow, not just because he is God, but because he was human – not just because he is without sin, but because he was also tempted.

Doubt: The First Step into Deconstruction

Doubt within the Christian faith can be a time of great anguish. It can also be very lonely. Oftentimes, due to fear, the doubter is left to deal with the struggle on their own because they don't want people to think that they are weak. And in some evangelical contexts that is exactly how they would be perceived.

However, doubt is not an attribute of the weak, but rather it demonstrates the mental fortitude of the strong. Doubt demonstrates a person's ability to critically think. And within their critical thinking, they may discover something about their belief that makes them feel uneasy. Sometimes one can identify what those incongruities are and sometimes it's just a feeling. Regardless, the willingness to confront those feelings takes great strength—and faith. This uneasiness is often why some people prefer not to critically think about their faith at all.

Throughout the history of Christianity, the idea of doubt has been presented as something antithetical to faith. Even today many preach the idea that doubting foundational Christian beliefs is a sin. In their view, doubt is a slippery slope, a dangerous idea that could easily make the doubter spiral into a nihilistic rabbit hole.

I have heard many church leaders using language that positions doubt in opposition to being a Christian; that when a person encounters doubt, they should deny it; that you cannot have doubt and faith at the same time. This is a misunderstanding of the nature of faith. I believe we should not flee from doubt, but run towards it, embrace it, and confront it for what it is.

Doubt is a psychological mechanism humans have to evaluate the probable truthfulness of propositions. For the philosopher Descartes, doubt was so fundamental to human existence that he believed it was the only thing that could not be denied. In other words, to doubt is to know that you exist. *Cogito, ergo sum.* Descartes believed doubt was the chief constituent of knowledge about the self and the world around it.

For Christians, doubt should not be viewed as negative, but as a positive protective mechanism that helps us to evaluate what we hear, read, and how we practice our faith. When people tell us not to doubt, what they are saying is that we should not evaluate our beliefs; that we should blindly accept what we have been told.

In reality, the opposite is true - our beliefs are defined and strengthened through doubt. Many of us avoid doubt because we are afraid of what it will do to our deeply held convictions. How often do we cycle back through some of our core theological beliefs and re-evaluate them? Not very often, if ever, for many of us. The reason is likely the fear that a long-held belief may turn out to be incorrect. This fear often results in panic and a desperate attempt to explain it away when we encounter something that sounds reasonable but contradicts something we already believe.

When Christians are confronted with major religious doubts, they are oftentimes unprepared for the psychological experience because the Church has failed to practice doubt as a spiritual discipline. As a result, when doubt sets in, many turn away from God instead of toward him. It's even worse for those who attend churches that actively preach against doubt. We must remember that doubt is not the enemy—blind adherence to what one has been taught is.

Doubt can also lead to depression. The reason for this is two-fold. First, such thinking can stagnate. We stew in the idea that ultimately our beliefs really don't matter. This is a dangerous way of thinking that can quickly cause one to spiral out of control. To avoid this trap, our thinking must always be moving forward.

Second, we lose the comfort of our certainty. For so long, many of us were taught by religious leaders to think in binary categories whereby something is either right or wrong, true or false, good or evil. Doubt and critical thinking reveal that we are really caught in the truth that the world is not black and white but filled with all colors of the spectrum.

Doubt is the preamble to deconstruction; it is the reason we do it. In his book, *Faith After Doubt,* Brian McLaren says:

> Only doubt can save the world. Only doubt will open a doorway out of hostile orthodoxies – whether religious, cultural, economic, or political. Only through the difficult passage of doubt can we emerge into a new stage of faith and a new regenerative way of life. Everything depends on making this passage.[11]

In Pursuit of Truth: Deconstruction

Those who approach evangelicalism with any type of critical thinking will eventually find themselves in a seemingly never-ending cycle of doubt. They will feel a sense of dread when doubt approaches. For those unequipped to handle such a situation, this can result in a total abandonment of the faith—and for many it does. These individuals confuse doubt with truth. For them, their doubt is their truth. Doubt is not meant to be experienced this way. Instead, doubt is meant to be understood as our first step into truth—we are not there yet. I have seen far too many evangelicals transition from doubt to atheism. Most of the time this happens because they have lived in absolutism for so long that any logical argument against a core belief can lead them to atheism. They live in an either/or, black and white world. It's all they've ever known. They fail to consider that even though their specific belief about something was not correct, perhaps there is a different belief not far off that is. The doubter cannot know this until they go through a deconstruction/reconstruction process.

Doubt for an evangelical almost inevitably leads to the need for deconstruction. Those individuals who wish to continue in their pursuit of truth begin that process. The loss of identity that occurs with deconstruction is the greatest fear of many who contemplate that path. Everyone deconstructing goes through this process as the traditional beliefs they once held so tightly are slowly destroyed through doubt. The foundation that once supported their house of beliefs becomes insecure, threatening the collapse of the whole structure.

Instead, the deconstructionist should go brick by brick, carefully examining each belief. This is important because not all beliefs will be incorrect, and some may just need rearticulation. It is not a helpful mindset for moving forward when one assumes that all they have learned up to that point in their life is incorrect simply because the source (for example, evangelicalism) is grounded in a fallacious way of thinking. It is this same exaggerated mindset that often leads one to accept absolutism to begin with.

The first step in the process of deconstruction is accepting the fact that some portion, if not all, of one's past identity, may be lost. Accepting this fact is not easy and can cause an identity crisis if one attempts to try and straddle two different worlds. Deconstruction must be done in a theological vacuum. In other words, one must get rid of their preconceived ideas for truth to reveal itself.

In Pursuit of Truth: Reconstruction

Within the dread of doubt and deconstruction, there is hope. This hope rests upon the knowledge that there will be a time of reconstruction, a time of optimistic rebuilding, a time of healing, and a time where the theological void will once again be filled. However, instead of filling your faith with unsubstantiated beliefs, it will be filled with the truth that has been discovered through the deconstruction and reconstruction process.

Many people skip the reconstruction process because they become so hopeless during the deconstruction phase. Some people are theologically exhausted after deconstruction and don't want to take the time to reconstruct. However, a building cannot re-build itself. If an individual takes the time to deconstruct, they should also take the time to reconstruct; otherwise, deconstruction leaves a deep void within them. I have found that many who have deconstructed themselves into atheism fall into this category.

Deconstruction and reconstruction are hallmarks of progressive Christianity. It makes sense that deconstruction is one of the primary targets for evangelicals to criticize since the majority of evangelicals who deconstruct end up leaving evangelicalism. However, much of the criticism is not based on facts but is conjecture that is created out of a general frustration over the shortcomings of evangelicalism itself.

WE WILL EXPLORE SOME of these shortcomings in the subsequent chapters, but our focus will not (and should not) be solely on the past. We must create a strong foundation to rebuild upon because the current evangelical foundation is broken and tattered. This foundation is built on a man-made perspective of the Bible, which we will dive into in the next chapter.

Evangelicals are not the only social antagonists. To be fair, there exists a similar social antagonism and activism within progressive thinking as well. Progressives tend to side more with liberal social issues than conservative ones. Ultimately, it comes down to a difference of opinion on what constitutes important social reform for the Church and what does not. With that said, I would argue that all social programs are important for the Church to understand and consider regardless of their political persuasion. Political persuasion is the real issue here because many have conflated the Kingdom of God and the kingdom of man, which makes it difficult for people to draw lines of distinction between the two.

Deconstruction helps rid us of any allegiances we have to the kingdom of man and unites us under the umbrella of the Kingdom of God. UNenlightening oneself does not have to be a painful task. It can be an enjoyable learning experience. It does not have to be a time of autonomy. During deconstruction, I recommend people surround themselves with people that they trust. These don't have to be people they know in person. In today's age of social media, they may find a community of deconstructed people that can come alongside and support them on their journey.

It is important as one deconstructs to foster good habits. One such habit is to stop listening to and reading people with whom you always agree. This echo chamber is detrimental to one's ability to develop critical thinking skills. Critical thinkers look at all sides of an issue before coming to a conclusion. It is the long road to truth, but it is the road we must take.

I also recommend that individuals get comfortable with mystery. In many conservative circles, it is common to claim that one has a divine-like knowledge of truth. Stating that something is a mystery is often viewed as a weakness, when in fact, it is just the opposite. Acknowledging mystery gives a head nod towards truth by admitting that it is beyond the capacity for humans to know. It is better to embrace a real sense of uncertainty and the mystery that oftentimes comes with it than it is to possess a false sense of certainty.

DISCUSSION QUESTIONS

1. Do you think that Christendom is a problem in the United States? If so, how have you seen it displayed?

2. Do you think systematic theology helps or harms one's understanding of theology? Think of examples when you've seen this happen.

3. Have you ever experienced doubt related to your faith? If so, what led you to doubt? How did your doubt evolve over time?

4. Have you ever participated in deconstruction or reconstruction of your faith? If so, what was your experience like.

5. How do you feel about the mystery of God? Are you comfortable or uncomfortable with the idea?

2

THE BIBLE, HEREMENEUTICS & TRUTH

"The Bible is a human product: it tells us how our religious ancestors saw things, not how God sees things."
— **Marcus Borg**

"I take the Bible far too seriously to take it literally."
— **Karl Barth**

THE BIBLE IS THE most unique and beautiful piece of literature on the planet. It comprises 66 books of various types of literature, such as poetry, history, music, letters, and biographies. It might be obvious that a book comprising such diverse literary interests might result in a struggle to unify how it is understood. The Church is at yet another crossroads as it becomes more and more divided on what the Bible means for Christians in today's culture.

The way people read the Bible is changing. Not because the Bible or God has changed, but because culture has. The traditional way to read the Bible that many grew up with is archaic and unpersuasive to many Christians. The rise of progressive Christianity illustrates a growing desire for a new way to understand the Christian Scriptures. Christians need a way that helps them interpret the Bible the way it was intended—without forcing modern presuppositions upon the text.

There is something freeing when you can throw off the old yoke of archaic methodologies and read Scripture anew or, as Marcus Borg puts it, "reading it again for the first time." Borg sums up this issue nicely:

> Reading and seeing go together. On the one hand, what we read can affect how we see. On the other hand, and more important for my immediate purpose, how we see affects how we read. What we bring to our reading of a text or document affects how we read it. All of us, whether we use reading glasses or not, read through lenses . . . We need a new set of lenses through which to read the Bible. The older set, ground and polished by modernity, no longer works . . .[1]

Perhaps no theological issue is greater or has more at stake than how we interpret the Bible. Very few things get progressives and evangelicals as heated as the issue of the Bible and its relationship to truth. Many progressives are frustrated over the lack of hermeneutical integrity evangelical theologians have when it comes to their understanding of Scripture. One primary example is their desire to preserve the doctrine of inerrancy above truth itself. Evangelical theologians have become so dependent upon inerrancy that much of their theology suffers as a result of it. In fact, it is these same hermeneutic principles that have led to interpretations of Scripture that have been used as fodder to ostracize and spiritually abuse others.

The most notable example of this is how poorly women are treated by many within evangelicalism and how evangelicals have used Scripture to justify this treatment. In some cases, male-dominated power structures have led to the abuse of women—as seen by the ongoing revelations of sexual assaults and harassment by clergy towards female congregants. This is especially an issue within evangelicalism where sexist mindsets drive power dynamics.[2] These stories of abuse are particularly appalling given that is likely just the tip of the iceberg since most experiences of abuse and harassment go unreported. These abuses illustrates how one's theology has a real-world impact on the wellbeing of others.

Evangelicals often accuse progressives of interpreting Scripture in a way that justifies progressive social beliefs, such as universalism and affirming non-heteronormative relationships. Evangelicals view progressives as superficial, flimsy Bible interpreters who do not take Scripture seriously enough. However, nothing could be farther from the truth. Some of the most spiritually impressive thinkers I have encountered have been progressive thinkers. Thinkers like Peter Rollins, Rob Bell, Richard Rohr, Pete Enns, Brian McLaren, Marcus Borg, Walter Brueggemann; and historical writers like Soren Kierkegaard (the archetype of a progressive thinker), Karl Barth, and H. Richard Niebuhr, to name just a few. There are also lesser-known thinkers like Rachel Held Evans, Kathryn Tanner, Dianna Butler Bass, etc.

To understand why progressives believe certain things about the Bible, it is important to first understand and agree upon the history. People often view history as objective, and yet it seems almost impossible to agree upon a single narrative. One of the reasons for this is that history is often treated the same way Scripture is treated. That is, people cherry-pick through history to create a narrative that suits them but is often more fiction than truth. It is important to resist the urge to do this in our pursuit of the truth.

The Bible

It is critical to first understand that the Bible is a compilation of various types of literature and can be overwhelming to one unaccustomed to its format and style. However, there is no disputing that it is a powerful piece of literature, evidenced by the more than five billion+ copies printed—far more than any other book, religious or otherwise. The Bible details both the triumphs and terrors of a people who followed—or neglected to follow—God through various circumstances. The Bible is not a book written by the winners but is comprised of stories that characterize disobedient, lawless people who abandoned their God for power and riches. I believe this adds to its legitimacy as a historical work regarding a people and their culture.

The Bible demands to be taken seriously. We must respect the various aspects of its contents. As such, we cannot understand such a diverse body of literature with a single lens. Instead, we must understand that approaching various contents differently (depending on the type of literature it is) does not dilute the truth but rather allows the truth to rise to emerge.

The Bible makes bold and audacious claims about humanity, God, and God's relationship to humanity. Perhaps the most remarkable aspect of the Bible is its ability to appeal to people from all different walks of life. The Bible can change an individual's perspective and purpose in life, as well as provide the thinker with philosophical musings to ponder for the extent of their life.

The Bible is one of the most controversial subjects that evangelicals and progressive Christians discuss. Evangelicals and progressives find a lot of uncommon ground when it comes to Scripture - from disagreeing on issues like inerrancy to arguing over the language we use to describe the Bible. It is important to first agree on hermeneutics in order to discuss the Bible since most progressive Christians complain that evangelicals misunderstand it or interpret it anachronistically.

What many literalists fail to understand is that the Bible can be read factually without being read literally. What's more, facts can be extrapolated from myths and truth from fantastical biographies. *The truth of Scripture cannot and should not be reduced to single propositions.* We should embrace the dynamism that is brought forth by the text itself and take dynamic approaches to understand its complexity.

The first question many ask about the development of the Bible is about the extent to which God was involved in the transmission process. Did God dictate the words of Scripture through human writers (the most conservative view), or did God simply inspire the human writers (a more liberal view)? Was God's involvement in the forming of Scripture equal between the inclusion of the Hebrew Scriptures and the New Testament? Should we simply trust that Jewish leaders formed their canon correctly, or do we trust that God was a part of that process as well? What about the Pseudepigrapha? Why don't we give the Pseudepigrapha the same weight as Jewish people do?[3]

The best-kept secret in evangelicalism is that much of how evangelicals view the Bible is relatively modern and does not have the ancient precedent that many believe it does. Even though evangelicalism is confessional in nature, its foundation is firmly rooted in the Reformation of the 1500s and not in the Early Church Fathers.[4] There is nothing inherently wrong with being rooted in the Reformation. However, the problem occurs when people are taught that foundational tenets of their faith are a part of ancient truth—a part of orthodoxy.

A Brief History of the Bible

There were already hundreds of scriptures circulating throughout the Ancient Near East (ANE) and beyond by 325 CE when the first council at Nicaea was formed. Between gnostic writings and other Pseudepigraphal works, it was difficult to distinguish between authentic and inauthentic writings. Constantine, the Emperor of Rome from 312-337 CE, and a convert to Christianity, believed it would be useful to have a single collection of scriptures for church unity. He commissioned and sponsored 50 Bibles to be created in 331 CE. These were the first Bibles the Church would use. Unfortunately, these copies have all been lost to history so we cannot be assured as to what scriptures were compiled. It's also likely that many of the books contained in this version were different than what is in the Christian Bible today—though some would have been the same.

It was not until Easter of 367 CE that Athanasius[5] produced a letter naming the current 27 books of the New Testament.[6] It took another fifty years of debate before the ratification of those 27 books was agreed upon by both the Eastern and Western churches. The oldest surviving Bible that is similar to the one that many protestants possess now is referred to as the Codex Sinaiticus. This Bible was produced sometime between 325 and 360 CE.[7] However, it is the Codex Alexandrinus[8] (400-440 CE) that is the closest to today's Christian Bible.

This anecdote testifies to the complex history of the New Testament's compilation. It also serves as an important reminder that more than 400 years passed after the earthly life of Jesus with no agreed upon "Bible" as we know it today. There were numerous scriptural manuscripts that circulated after the crucifixion of Jesus, some of which ended up in our modern Bible and some that did not. Even when the Bible was compiled, only churches owned them and only Bishops were privy to its contents. It wasn't until the invention of the printing press and the subsequent Reformation that the Bible became available to the public. That means it took around 1,500 years after Jesus's death for laypeople to have access to a Bible. What's more, it was not until the mid-1800s before a Bible was produced that resembles the one in wide circulation today.

The Bible has become an idol in today's hyper-biblical evangelicalism. It is the golden calf of our age. What was meant to inform the Christian faith has instead replaced Jesus in the hierarchy of importance. Christians call the

Bible "the Word of God" and many claim it is inerrant, perfect in what it communicates. Unfortunately, like its history, it is not that simple.

Biblical Inerrancy

The majority of evangelicals hold to the inerrancy of Scripture. Evangelicals often use the Chicago Statement on Inerrancy to define biblical inerrancy. Evangelical Wayne Grudem summarizes it this way: "Scripture in the original manuscripts does not affirm anything contrary to fact."[9] The term "original manuscripts" is a misnomer because even though we don't have the original manuscripts, we do have enough of the older manuscripts to know that what we have in our current Bibles is largely the same text that the original manuscripts contained.

Evangelicals cannot imagine a world where the Bible can be both from God and not inerrant at the same time. However, one is not contingent upon the other. If God actually *dictated* the Bible, then there is an argument to be made that Scripture is inerrant. However, God did not dictate Scripture. Most evangelicals would even concede this point. God *influenced* Scripture because he used humans to convey his message. This message goes through the fallible human before it is transmitted into manuscript form. God did not whisper in the ear of the writer. God used various methods to communicate with people, not unlike what he does today. Therefore, the Bible cannot possibly be inerrant due to the fallibility of the middleman. To believe that humans have the power to communicate Divine Truth without compromising its integrity means that humans have the capabilities of being Divine.

I believe there are three good arguments against the doctrine of inerrancy. First, it lacks any Early Church historical precedence. Second, there is the problem of inspiration. Finally, there is the canon problem. None of these taken by themselves serve as a good argument, but when taken together, they create a persuasive argument against the *likelihood* that biblical inerrancy is true. I dive deeper into these arguments in the sections below.

The Historicity of Biblical Inerrancy

Unlike what many evangelical scholars argue, inerrancy is not an ortho-dox doctrine, but a relatively new phenomenon. Although some argue that something similar can be found in the writings of Augustine,[10] belief in inerrancy does not become a widespread belief until the Middle Ages.[11] In fact, one could argue that the idea of Scripture being inerrant was of such little importance to the Early Church that it is not mentioned in any creed or any writings they produced.

What's more, a parallel can be drawn between the rise in scientific un-derstanding and the increase in the widespread belief in inerrancy. It only becomes an important issue for the early-20th century fundamentalists who were desperate to compete with the scientific worldview, which they viewed as a threat to their belief system. Once fundamentalism joined evangelical-ism, the doctrine of inerrancy became widely accepted within conservative Christianity.

The Inspiration Problem

In order for inerrancy to be true, it must also be the case that those who eventually canonized Scripture were under the same inspiration as the writers of the Scriptures were. Otherwise, there would be no way for them to know which scriptures out of the hundreds of writings available at that time were the inspired ones.

It is important to note that those who participated in the organization of Scripture did not believe they were inspired by God. Instead, they believed they were taking part in a logical process used to determine which books were beneficial for the Church. Their process was simple: 1) Did the author have first-hand knowledge of the information they presented (AKA a disciple or apostle)? 2) Does the book have provenance (e.g., was the Gospel of Thomas actually written by Thomas, and can we verify that?)

Unfortunately, hidden in the subconscious of many of the bishops who presided over the councils was the intention of ensuring that the scriptures they chose aligned with accepted doctrine. Not everyone present agreed on which books fell into this category. In fact, even as late as the 1500s, Martin Luther[12] believed that some books were less inspired than others or not inspired at all.

Furthermore, the Protestant Bible took several hundred years to compile making it unlikely that those who took part in this process were inspired by God. It is more likely that God allowed those involved to use reasoning and a systematic process to make the decisions about which scriptures should be included in the canon.

The Canon Problem

We are left with the final issue for inerrancy, which is the canon problem. Even if we assume the previous problems don't exist, we are stuck with the question, "Which canon is the inerrant one?"

There is more than one version of the Bible. In fact, the version that most Protestants use is relatively new; it is not the version codified by the Early Church. That version is used by Catholic Christians. The Protestant version was not formed until the mid-19th century.

There also exist other canons that contain different books. There is the Roman Catholic version (Latin, Western), the Protestant version, the Orthodox version (Greek, Eastern), the Oriental Orthodox version, and the Ethiopian version, just to name a few.

As I stated in the previous chapter, the issue of inerrancy is dangerous because it acts as the foundation for all evangelical hermeneutics. This doctrine can oftentimes create false-positive propositions. In other words, certain ideas or even facts are often ignored if they come in conflict with inerrancy.

For many evangelicals, it is more important to preserve inerrancy or specific doctrines than it is to prove the truth of Scripture.

The Bible as the Word of God?

Is the Bible the Word of God? This is the "authority" question that is primary between progressives and evangelicals. To understand what is meant by "Word," we need to first understand how the term functioned in the original language. Two Greek words are used for the term "Word." The first is *rhema*. This is used most often to denote what we commonly understand to be typical forms of communication, such as: language, speech, conversations, etc.

The second term that is used is *logos*. This word is a bit more complicated as it has a long philosophical history. Therefore, to play it safe, I will define it conservatively. The best example of how the term functions is shown in the familiar passage John 1:1: *"In the beginning was the Word, and the Word was with God, and the Word was God"* (emphasis mine).

In Stoicism, the term logos is used in conjunction with what Stoics called "Divine Reason." This is the idea that the only true divine philosophy must co-exist with action. The definition most commonly associated with logos is "revelation" or "to make known." Therefore, a proper reading of John 1:14 "...the Word became flesh..." forces us to understand the Divine Logos this way: Jesus came to "reveal" God through the "action" of the Incarnation (and later his life, death, and resurrection.) Many biblical scholars believe John borrows the term logos from its stoic function.

Evangelicals will point to various passages within Scripture that claim it is the Word of God, such as 2 Timothy 3:16: ". . . All Scripture is God-breathed useful for teaching, rebuking, correcting, and training in righteousness . . ."

Or Hebrews 4:12,

"For the *word of God* is alive and active. Sharper than any double-edged sword, it penetrates even to dividing soul and spirit, joints and marrow; it judges the thoughts and attitudes of the heart" (emphasis mine).

Or 2 Corinthians 2:17, "Unlike so many, we do not peddle the word of God for profit. On the contrary, in Christ, we speak before God with sincerity, as those sent from God."

The problem with not only these passages, but any passage that points to Scripture being the Word of God, is that these passages are not about the Bible. The Bible had not yet been codified, so when passages refer to the "Word of God," they are referencing various meanings depending on the context. Most of the time they are in reference to the Torah. Based on this, there is no reasonable way to use a self-authentication argument when it comes to answering the question, is the Bible the Word of God?

A Third Perspective: The Holy Spirit

Theologians talk a lot about the "illumination" of Scripture by the Holy Spirit. Illumination happens when an individual is reading Scripture and the Holy Spirit reveals truths to them through the text. The logical extension of this is to argue that the Bible becomes the Word of God at the point when the Holy Spirit illuminates truth to the believer. It is not the Word of God until this illumination process occurs.

The belief that the Bible *becomes* the Word of God is often associated with Neo-Orthodoxy. Neo-Orthodoxy is defined by the way it holds to particular theological traditions while at the same time imagining them in new and invigorating ways. Theologians like Karl Barth, H. Richard Niebuhr, and Paul Tillich are often described as Neo-Orthodox because of their emphasis on the dynamic nature of revelation as the primary source for Christian doctrine. Progressives often echo this sentiment because of their belief that God is a dynamic, active deity that is intimately involved in the lives of humanity. If one truly believes in the spiritual authority of Scripture, then they must concede that believers and unbelievers view it differently. If they view it differently, then the Bible cannot be the Word of God in and of itself, but must, in some way transform when the believer accesses its spiritual truths.

The Problem of Propositionalism

The problems associated with systematic theology were covered in the previous chapter. However, I want to go deeper into the troubling relationship systematic theology has to propositionalism. We have postliberal theologian George Lindbeck (1923-2018) to thank for the link between evangelical theology and propositionalism. Lindbeck referred to evangelical theological methods as the "cognitive-propositional approach."[13] Propositionalism is the reduction of biblical ideas to manageable propositions that are then organized into theological loci.

Propositionalism presupposes that language can arrange itself in such a way that propositions retain their meaning despite the surrounding context to the contrary. In other words, an individual can extract propositional content from the Bible, and it can stand alone as its own truth even if the context contradicts that truth. Propositions are not negative in and of themselves, but they rarely line up nicely with predefined categories. This is why people have gone to great lengths to create narrative-based theological perspectives that better encompasses the way the Bible speaks to us. Narrative-based approaches take into consideration the literary style as well as the contextual facts that accompany each text.

Propositionalism also eliminates or seriously reduces the necessity of action. Belief is static in a propositionalist worldview. The action of *belief* is all that is necessary for the proposition to be true. Unfortunately, this perspective ignores the Christian's calling to *be* a certain way, not to just *believe* a certain way. Christians are called to *live* this truth in front of the world.[14]

Propositionalism cannot support this expressive requirement because it is solely reliant on cognition.

The dangers of propositionalism have real-world consequences as we have seen. Scripture has been propositionalized in order to make certain claims that align with the readers preferences. Pastors teach this way of understanding Scripture to their congregations because they were taught this way by the seminaries that educated them. Even children are taught this way of thinking in and throughout evangelical churches – especially those who rely on a curriculum they have not created. Propositionalism is engrained in the evangelical consciousness.

Unfortunately, regardless of the truthfulness of their propositions, some propositionalists have used their methods to harm and ostracize people with whom they disagree. Propositionalists can justify just about any belief under their rules for biblical interpretation. This is not only dangerous but truly heretical in the most obscene sense.

The Nature of Truth and the Bible

The Bible is the foundation for the Christian faith, not the foundation for truth. A "literal" understanding of Scripture does not mean that the words are understood plainly, but that the ideas are understood as they were intended to be understood. This requires us to take the time to understand the writer and their context so that we can have a *real* literal understanding of what is being said. The progressive view takes Scripture seriously enough that it refuses to take it at word value, but cares to take the time to understand the full narrative within its context.

Sometimes understanding the Bible literally, means that we understand it figuratively if that was the intent of the author. Whether or not we are reading a text accurately is fully contingent upon whether or not we are reading it as it was intended to be read. To read something out of context as fodder for some argument is not taking the text literally, it is reading it inaccurately.

The purpose of the Bible is not to be a metaphysical treatise on truth. Those making lofty claims about God that are not true, take away from the miraculous times when they are true. Many within evangelicalism fail to understand that the truth of the Bible is no different than the truth they experience every day in the "real world." It need not change once we begin reading the Bible.

This lack of understanding truth is often due to a fundamental misunderstanding regarding the nature of truth as it relates to God. Evangelicals believe that humans can understand "(T)ruth" from a Being higher than themselves. However, this is not possible unless we think we are in some way coequal to this Higher Being. This is not to say that we cannot know "(t)ruth." We can observe parts of truth, which means those parts are in and of themselves true, but we are not able to view truth in its entirety—(T)ruth. If we could, we would not need God.

Absolutism, Certainty, & Subjectivity

Modernist thinking presupposes the absolutism of truth. It also views truth as static and not dynamic. In other words, humanity exists in a closed system uninfluenced by anything metaphysical (because metaphysics doesn't even exist in a Hegelian worldview.) This is an important concept to understand because it presupposes that anything metaphysical must actually be treated as physical.

The presupposition of this closed system allows for philosophers (like Hegel) to assert that absolute truth is possible through a dialectical methodology[15] created specifically to ascertain the possibility of all truth. This foundation created by Hegel was later used to develop the scientific method.

As explained in the previous chapter, Hegel's method for ascertaining absolute truth can be understood through three concepts: thesis, antithesis, and synthesis. The thesis is the initial proposition that is under consideration. Hegel believed that if one submitted that thesis to its opposite (antithesis), one could come up with the actual truth of the proposition they originally submitted (synthesis). Although, for some reason, Hegel believed one had to do this three times to get at the actual truth. It's not entirely clear why three is the magic number. Subsequent philosophers have argued that you simply reduce the proposition until it becomes irreducible.

One can begin to see how dangerous this method is for theology since theology is built upon the premise of a metaphysical God. And yet, evangelicalism has largely adopted this worldview because they like the idea of having a Christianity that is absolute. They like the idea that their faith can exist within the comfort of certainty.

Ironically, certainty is a temptation that is hard to resist and yet we must if we wish to find the truth. Certainty depends on objectivity, which as humans, we are not fully able to experience. The goal of deconstruction is not a total annihilation of objectivity, but a reframing of its exclusive relationship to truth. Ultimately, objectivity provides an important scientific framework. It's when this is applied to theology that it becomes a problem.

This particular principle is vitally important to discuss because many Christians believe that the truth of Christianity *has* to be objective and absolute for it to be true. This is a fallacious way of thinking that is so ingrained in our churches that it has become axiomatic to many. It is also the case that many scientists have the same requirement for determining truth for a religion. We must be just as outspoken to that group as well. Objectivity is not an appropriate way of thinking when it comes to the metaphysics of religion.

The desire Christians often have for absolutism comes out of our need to prove the existence of God to skeptics who, by the way, often believe in the absolutism of truth as well. However, what is really happening is that many are just trying to prove God to themselves more than to the skeptics. Sometimes Christians can be their own worst skeptic. We have to learn how to trust our subjectivity. Subjectivity is what fostered belief for the ancient Israelites and the Early Church. Each group certainly had a unique relationship with God that was purely subjective. Unfortunately, the belief that people have minds capable of fully objective thought regarding the metaphysical, has overshadowed the unique relationship subjectivity has with truth.

Consider for a moment a few questions: Why does truth have to be absolute? Why can't it be subjective? Who has imposed this restriction on us? Do we not stand before a Holy God who, in his nature, is absolute truth? Does it not mean then that when we look at the absolute, we are doing so from our subjective vantage points? Is not my experience of the absolute God, subjective? It seems the height of arrogance to believe that we can put ourselves on the same level as God. This is a sin. We are not God! And when we try to act like God, it does nothing but drive us farther from his presence.

Christians can memorize verses and arguments for the existence of God, but it will not deepen their faith—even though they have increased their knowledge. Instead, it creates a dangerously shallow faith that is built upon an insecure foundation, a foundation that when challenged will quickly buckle under the weight of true self-examination. Too many Christians have bought into the idea that more knowledge equals greater faith. We have to keep in mind that *knowing* and *being* are two different things. They must inform each other so that wisdom can prevail, but this must not come at the exclusion of the other.

There is a legitimate practical problem for the individual who embraces the idea that their faith is absolute. That is, they rarely reconsider that their foundational beliefs are anything but true. They are stuck in a closed worldview where they do not need help to refine their faith. Why listen to anyone who believes differently? They are far too willing to trust those to whom they have given authority over their lives. They forget how or never learn to think for themselves.

The reason deconstruction can be so destructive is because it interferes with the individual's idea of certainty. Their line of thinking is often: "...if this small thing is now questionable, then what does that mean for the larger more significant beliefs down the line?" This slippery slope can be terribly unnerving for an individual. There are only certain types of people who can rebound from such an encounter with the truth.

Unfortunately, I think belief in this absolutism is largely due to an inability to understand what it means for God to be "Absolute Truth." Or perhaps it has something to do with our arrogance to think we can comprehend such a truth completely. Ultimately, the idea of absolutism cannot hold together under the weight of its own criteria. In other words, objectivity cannot prove itself using its own methodology. Ironically, Hegel's system requires the subjectivity of a human to render it.

God is the only thing that is absolute. God is both objective and subjective.[16] He is the only one able to perceive himself with the confidence of certainty. As purely subjective humans, we are fallible when it comes to our perceptions of truth. We can only gaze upon parts of the absolute and do our best to communicate that to the world. That does not mean we cannot ascertain truth, because the parts that we can see are enough for us to exist within.

THE BIBLE IS A beautiful, yet complicated piece of literature. The Bible does not take a single form but comprises many different types of literature. Therefore, it should be interpreted with the humility and grace that Scripture requires—especially if we believe they were inspired in some way by God!

As Christians, we need to increase our biblical literacy without falling into the trap of making Scripture exclusive. We need to understand that God reveals himself to humanity through a variety of ways, none of which is exclusive to the Bible. We need to foster all of the ways that God reveals himself to us with the same passion and zeal that we have for the Bible. God is not dead. He is still active in the believer's life. If we truly believe this, then it should be demonstrated by our actions.

DISCUSSION QUESTIONS

1. What is your origin story? Is there anything unique about your story? How does your origin give insight into who you are now?

2. What is your view on the Bible (inerrancy, inspiration, etc.), and what has informed your beliefs?

3. Do you think propositionalism is a problem? How have you seen it used in the Church?

4. What is your view of truth? Can we know it? Is it absolute or subjective?

5. Do you think we can have certainty with our beliefs? If so, what gives you assurance?

3

GOD: THE DIVINE MIND & THE (F)ATHER: THE DIVINE WILL

"To fall in love with God is the greatest romance; to seek him the greatest adventure; to find him, the greatest human achievement."
— **Saint Augustine**

"If I am capable of grasping God objectively, I do not believe, but precisely because I cannot do this I must believe."
— **Soren Kierkegaard**

IT IS IN GOD that we live, move, and have our being.[1] God exists in a great boundless love that permeates throughout all creation. The very act of creating the cosmos was based upon this love. Perhaps even greater is the love God expressed in enfleshing the "son" to live among the creation and leaving the Spirit to guide us in this life. The great love that God possesses is demonstrated in the acts of love that we as humans display towards others. "We love because God first loved us!"[2]

You might wonder about the purpose of a complicated doctrine like the Trinity. Well, we have Jesus to thank for that. Judaism is a monotheistic religion; they worship a single God whom they refer to as YAHWEH. When the Incarnation occurred, it caused an intellectual and spiritual inconsistency. The question that Jesus forced the religious leaders of his time (and the Early Church Fathers) to consider was, "How could the God of the universe Incarnate himself? Were there really two Gods? Or was there one God who simply abandoned his place in Heaven to be with humans?"

For the religious leaders of the time, there was no way that Jesus could have been God. Maybe a prophet, but certainly not an eternal deity. For the Early Church Fathers, their task became trying to understand how Jesus, the father, and the Holy Spirit's relationship worked. The Early Church Fathers committed a lot of time debating this issue and trying to articulate a formula that made sense. How could three unique entities all somehow be God and still exist within a monotheist religion?

After several hundred years, a formula was developed that helped to make sense of this complicated issue. The formula that the Early Church Fathers developed is still used today by most Christians to understand the Trinity. It goes a little something like this: God is one consubstantial being (*homoousia*) who consists of three co-eternal, co-equal persons (*hypostases*).[3] The nature of God describes *what* God is, whereas personhood describes *who* the father, son, and Holy Spirit are.

The Trinity

The Trinity is complicated, and our language is limited in how we can communicate this unique idea. There may be times in this book where it appears that I am breaking the formula for the Trinity and theological ideas associated with this major doctrine. Much of what we talk about when it comes to the

Trinity is outside the existence of time. Moreover, when we use time-based language, it becomes difficult to communicate ideas about the Trinity while at the same time maintaining theological and philosophical integrity. Therefore, I am using what I refer to as "logical moments" to describe something like time intervals. These are imaginary moments outside of time where we can isolate the Trinity to make observations and claims about who God is.

Let's start with what I refer to as the *necessity* of triune persons. Necessity simply refers to the logical need for a thing to exist. Therefore, even though the Trinity has always been, we must still hit the "pause" button for a moment to discuss the necessity of it. With that said, regardless of the appearance that the language induces, the Trinity is eternal and unbegotten.[4]

The Trinity is probably one of the most unique philosophical idea that has ever been proposed. In fact, it is so unique that every analogy that is proposed falls short of actually describing the nature of God. Christianity's adherence to the aforementioned formula is probably the most orthodox belief presented in this entire book. The trinitarian formula is the only requirement for expressing some logical version of the Trinity. This means that it doesn't matter how we analogize the Trinity as long as we stick to the formula. We can know each individual role of the Trinity based on how it functions in the world.

There are various options to explain the nature of God that the Early Church considered when they debated the Trinity. Their view of Jesus heavily influenced how they weighed each option. For example, did Jesus always exist? Was Jesus born a person who somehow became God while on Earth? Was Jesus a demi-god? Was Jesus part of the creation or is he coeternal? Whatever they ultimately decided would determine how they formed trinitarian doctrine.

Progressive theologians have largely been silent about the doctrine of the Trinity. If progressive Christians believe in the Trinity, they would most likely use a social-based model to understand the Trinity's role and function since it comports nicely with their view of social justice. However, some combination of the social Trinity and Augustine's psychological Trinity is probably the most accurate way to view the nature of God. Both versions of the Trinity have, at their core, a relational nature that serves as an example of how human relationships not only exist but flourish.

Some of the trinitarian questions the Early Church had to consider were, "Are there three distinct deities?" "Does God take three separate forms depending on the circumstance, but there is always one God?" "Is 'God' just a term meant to describe a common attribute that three distinct persons share?" Ultimately, a more sophisticated version of the last option was decided on by the Early Church Fathers.

Augustine's psychological Trinity consists of one Divine Mind with three aspects: Memory, Understanding, and Will (*De Trinitate, Augustine*). I believe Augustine was on the right track. However, there is a disconnect between how he imagines two of the three persons. I agree with Augustine that the Trinity should be viewed as a Divine Mind in its oneness, but his argument that memory and understanding are necessary for a Divine Mind is awkward for a psychological Trinity. Perhaps Augustine's model is better described as a pedagogical model of the Trinity since his analogy is really about how a mind learns.

God: The Divine Mind

The best way to explore the nature of the Trinity is to determine what is logically necessary for it to exist. Of course, all theories must begin with a premise. Augustine's premise, as already stated, is that God is a Divine Mind. The question we must pose from here is, "What aspects of the mind would be necessary in order to have a Divine Mind actually exist?" The logical necessity of this Divine Mind extends to the persons that make up God.

Much of what is extrapolated below is based upon a tangential premise that since humanity is created in the image of God, there must be some aspects of humanity that resemble God. Humans are, at their core, *minds* and *bodies*.

Upon death, the mind and body are ripped apart so that the mind can fulfill its eternal destiny even as the earthly body decomposes. This must mean then that our minds are the primary aspect of our being. Therefore, it's not a huge leap to suggest that God's primary nature is also a Mind, since we were created in his image.

Humans have also been created for community. We are social beings and require socialization to thrive and feel a sense of belonging. The same could be said of the Trinity. There is a social aspect to the Trinity that goes beyond the communicative aspect of community. Therefore, there is a sense in which communal existence is necessary for the triune God and as such, it exists in three persons who share an eternal communal existence as a single being.

The Divine Attributes

God, or the Divine Mind, contains within itself certain attributes that are not only an aspect of its oneness, but that are also distributed equally to the individual persons of the Trinity. Although there are many attributes I could discuss, there are three, in particular, that I will focus on: Omnipotence, Omniscience, and Omnipresence.

Traditional theology has roughly defined these Divine attributes in the following ways:

Omnipotence – God is all-powerful.
Omniscience – God is all-knowing.
Omnipresence – God is everywhere.[5]

It is difficult to try to grasp the attributes of God. However, the way that Christians have traditionally understood them is problematic. In this current attribute model, there are logical inconsistencies between how God exists within his being and how we perceive God to exist. For example, if we say that God is all-powerful, it begs questions like, "Then why does he allow evil to exist in the world," or "Can he make a rock so big that he can't lift it?" Each of these has its own logical problems; however, we can solve this by simply using the inverse of the definition for each attribute:

Omnipotence – Nothing is more powerful than God.
Omniscience – Nothing happens outside of God's knowledge.
Omnipresence – Nothing exists outside of God's presence.

This reframing avoids the aforementioned logical inconsistencies, as well as simplifies the meaning behind one of the most complex theological doctrines within Christianity.

The Divine Mind's Nature

The Divine Mind is simple in its oneness. By simple, I mean that God is not divisible; God already exists in its simplest form. But the Divine Mind is also complex because it is incomprehensible. This may seem like a paradox, but it illustrates just how complicated the nature of God is and how difficult it is for humans to apprehend such a Being.

As a result, we develop analogies. Analogies are necessary to understand the nature of God (e.g., Divine Mind) so that we can have an image to associate with our adoration. However, if we try and imagine God as he really is, we fail. The same is true with our language. Our linguistic categories are insufficient to process what we experience as God. For example, for centuries humans have fallen into the trap of associating personal pronouns to describe God. There are two reasons for this: first, the analogies Jesus chose to use to describe the first person of the Trinity (e.g., father) lead us into thinking this way. Second, the fact that Jesus was born as a man. (I explore this further in the chapter on Jesus.) Third, Jesus describes his relationship to the "father" as being the "son."

The fact of the matter is that God is without sex or gender. This is the case because sex and gender would qualify as a limitation within a divine being. For the same reason we would say that God does not have a stomach – because he does not need to eat; or a bladder – because he does not need to urinate. All of these "human" necessities do not exist in God. The same could be said about gender. To be a man is a limitation because God would lack the importance of what it means to be a woman and vice versa. Therefore, out of the necessity that God does not have any weakness and must, in the end, be the greatest possible being, God must be nonbinary.

Our language is severely limited in attaching symbols to God. Therefore, we are stuck with using pronouns sometimes or redundantly saying "God" or "the Divine Mind" when communicating about God. Ultimately, in this book, I decided to use the former in a limited way; however, I have done my best to limit the use of pronouns to describe the persons of God and underemphasize gender when discussing God.

Eternal Subordination

Eternal subordination is the idea that the relationship between Jesus the "son" and God the "father" revealed a subordination as demonstrated by the titles "father" and "son." It further argues that this separation was not just while Jesus was upon the Earth, but that this differentiation is eternal. Jesus also appears to be subordinate to the father when it comes to accomplishing the father's Will over his own.[6]

Although eternal subordination has its roots in Arianism,[7] it has been in vogue for many years within evangelicalism. Eternal subordination has also been used to analogize the submission that should occur between a husband and a wife within complementarianism.[8] Complementarianism argues that men and women were created equal in their natures, but not in their roles, that the roles men and women have are meant to complement one another and not create a hierarchy. However, subordination is an example of a "role" that women have under this system. It doesn't take a philosopher to see the incongruity in the argument; by definition subordination is hierarchical.

Many evangelicals deny this is a heretical movement, desperate as they are to maintain their complementarian views of marriage. This is a rare move for evangelicals as they pride themselves on being orthodox and not heretical. However, some of them want to keep this relational power structure intact so badly they are willing to commit heresy to do so.

Any type of subordination, whether in nature or function, is inconsistent with trinitarian theology. Differentiation in roles does not entail any type of hierarchy unless your role is explicitly hierarchical (i.e., subordination). There are three distinct persons with individual functions within the trinitarian formula, which contribute to the overall functionality of the Divine Mind. However, in none of their functions can there be subordination because it creates a hierarchy, thus violating the trinitarian formula, which explicitly states that the persons are "coequal."

The Three Persons

As mentioned previously, each person of the Trinity exists out of necessity. In order to know what these persons resemble we can look at how each function within the Bible. At the very least, we know that the Divine Mind has a Will because it created the cosmos with purpose. The Divine Will (as represented by the father) is also explicitly mentioned throughout the Gospels.[9] Because we know that the Divine Mind has a Will, we also know there must be a way to express that purpose. The Divine Will is expressed through the Divine Word – Jesus - whose explicit purpose is to reveal the Divine Will to humanity. For a mind to know who and what it is, it must possess a sense of consciousness—it must be self-aware. The Holy Spirit, or what I refer to as the Divine Consciousness, acts as self-consciousness for the Divine Mind and links humanity and God together. These persons of the Trinity will be explained in a little more detail below. However, much of what needs to be said about them will be explained more fully in their respective sections of this book.

There exists a Divine Will as expressed by the Divine Word (Jesus) throughout the Gospels.[10] This Divine Will expresses a person who has planned how creation should operate. The Divine Will is the creative force behind the formation of the cosmos and contains so much power in their being that by mere proclamation, things come into existence. The "father" has willed creation into existence because he is, in his essence, Will.

Jesus should be understood as the Divine Word. The Divine Word is the main communicative voice for God. The Word is able to execute the Divine Will. He is the living revelation of God to the world. More will be said about Jesus as the Divine Word in the next chapter.

The Word and Will are linked together through a Divine Consciousness. This Divine Consciousness is also what links the human to God. For example, when we pray, the utterances are heard within the deep recesses of God. This Divine Consciousness has its own personhood based upon the necessity of its existence to link the Word and Will together within the Divine Mind. The believer has this unique connection to God through the Divine Consciousness and has been given the power to distribute that connection in their life.

One unique way that the Trinity expresses itself is through its concern for social justice. We know that the Trinity is concerned with social justice as it was a primary aspect of God's Will as expressed through the ministry of Jesus. It was also a main theme in the Hebrew Scriptures and demonstrated through the words and ministry of the prophets.

Traditional Heretical Views

There are two atypical expressions of the Trinity not covered thus far. (Subordinationism was covered earlier in this chapter.) The first expression is referred to as Modalism. This perspective states that there is one person who expresses themselves in three different forms. This perspective is largely in disrepute because it would mean that there was no Deity in Heaven when Jesus was on Earth. It also implies Jesus had some kind of dissociative identity disorder when he addresses the "father."

The second option would be to take off the restriction of monotheism and say there are three separate Gods. This is referred to as Tritheism. The classical view of the Trinity is oftentimes critiqued as being dressed up Tritheism.

Trinitarian Justice

There are two Trinitarian perspectives or aspects used to describe the Trinity's ontology. The first relates to the internal functions of the Divine Mind. I maintain that the Trinity is a social, Divine Mind comprised of a Divine Will, Word, and Consciousness. These persons act both independently and in sync with one another as a social community within the Divine Mind. Just as our mind has its own independent aspects, so too does the Divine Mind.

The second is related to their external social aspect. This is reflected not only throughout Scripture but in the lives of believers. Since we are created in the image of God (imago Dei), we inherit some of the Divine Mind's attributes, such as having a mind, our need for social relationships, etc. This inference is a direct reflection of the life of the Trinity.

The Trinity's primary concern with humanity is its expression of social justice in the world. All three persons of the Trinity have participated in these acts in their own unique way. We know that this is the case because it is a primary concern of the Old Testament, as well as the Gospel. The string that binds social justice together is love. To show concern for others is to express love towards God and his creation.

Many of the prophets spoke about social justice toward both Israel and Judah. Malachi 3:5 describes what will happen to Judah if they continue to deny social justice to their people.

So I will come to put you on trial. I will be quick to testify against sorcerers, adulterers and perjurers, against those who defraud laborers of their wages, who oppress the widows and the fatherless, and deprive the foreigners among you of justice.

Likewise, the following passages also demonstrate God's priority of justice:

Ezekiel 18:5-9: The righteous perform justice and prevent injustice.

Amos 5; 8:5: Much of this discusses how the Israelites take unfairly from the poor.

Jeremiah 22:15-16: Equates justice for the poor with being righteous and knowing what God desires.

Isaiah 1:17: Concern over oppression, widows, and single parents.

Zechariah 7:9-10: Concern over single parents, oppression, and the poor.

Few Old Testament scholars will argue with the fact that many of the prophets were concerned with social justice. Injustice was a significant complaint among those like Amos and Micha who saw the way the poor were treated as completely unacceptable. There is enough of an emphasis among the Prophets regarding social justice that we should take it seriously. It was this sin of Israel that Jesus called out several times because it was a problem even during his time. In this way, the prophets and Jesus are unified in their message and social calling.

It wasn't just the prophets of the Old Testament who were concerned about the social condition of the world. The Gospels are very clear that Jesus was concerned about the well-being of those he encountered, many of whom were quite poor. I am especially struck by the scene where Jesus opens the book of Isaiah to begin his ministry. The story is recorded in Luke 4:16-19:

"The Spirit of the Lord is on me because he has anointed me to proclaim good news to the poor. He has sent me to proclaim freedom to the prisoners and recovery of sight for the blind, to set the oppressed free, to proclaim the year of the Lord's favor."

Jesus started his ministry on a platform of social reform. Jesus could have chosen a passage about how he has come to set the captives free and bring Israel to its former glory —a real crowd-rousing speech. Instead, he chose to read a passage about social justice from the prophet Isaiah.

Jesus wasn't concerned about one particular social issue, but all of the social concerns of his day. This is evidenced by the fact that he helped a wide variety of people, from those needing physical healing to those needing spiritual healing. He not only demonstrated this throughout his life, but he also illustrates how concerned the Divine Will is with social justice because Jesus reflected the father's will.

If we are to assume that the Trinity is truly interested in justice, then it begs the question, "Why does God allow evil to befall good people?" It also requires us to wrestle with the question as to why God allows arbitrary suffering.

The Problem of Evil

One of the most common questions asked about God is, "Why does God allow suffering in the world?" This question is particularly acute when our loved ones suffer or there is a tragedy on a massive scale. This is often referred to as "the problem of evil." Humans have struggled with this question for millennia. The book of Job in the Hebrew Scriptures attempts to address this question in part by recounting the story of a "righteous and upright" man named Job. Job endures great suffering through the tragic loss of his entire family and estate. Despite this, he remains faithful and trusts in God's wisdom.

The moral of the story is that we cannot fathom the depths of God's wisdom and that when we suffer, it is for some inexplicable reason. There are other lessons the Jewish writer was trying to communicate through this story, such as: God will give back two-fold, all you have to have is faith, etc. However, none of these speak to the modern notion of suffering.

It could be argued that the issue of suffering is not just physical but can also be mental or spiritual. Why does God allow so many people to endure mental or spiritual suffering? This is one aspect of the story of Job that is not addressed – internal suffering. The war that Job waged in his mind with God is not detailed in the depth that would normally be experienced with suffering through such loss.

Regardless, the question of innocent suffering is the question of the problem of evil. Perhaps the most poignant example of innocent suffering, physically, mentally, and spiritually is the brutal death of Jesus Christ. Why did God allow his "son" to suffer as he did when God could have easily intervened? Jesus could have still died, but why did he have to "suffer"?

The underlying logic behind the problem of evil is that if God exists and is all-powerful and good, then why is there gratuitous evil in the world? Because evil does exist, then one of the following options must be true about God: (1) he is impotent to prevent evil (2) he doesn't care (3) he doesn't exist.

Presuppositions, like those we discussed in Chapter 1, often accompany discussions on the problem of evil and, as a result, prevent reconciliation of the matter. The question of the problem of evil is really multiple questions spanning various aspects of the human condition and experience. These assumptions are subsumed into the logic of the subsequent statements.

The Logical Problem

1. How does an all-powerful, good God allow gratuitous evil to exist in the world?

2. There exists gratuitous evil in the world.

3. Therefore, either God is impotent, doesn't care, or doesn't exist.[11]

Solutions for the Problem of Evil

A *theodicy* is an act of attempting to justify why evil exists in the world *despite the existence of a "good" God*. Many theodicies have been offered throughout history. Punishment theodicy, for example, argues that evil happens to people as a consequence of their own sinful actions. This belief was common in the ancient world, and unfortunately, this mindset is still very present today in American culture. In the 1980s, for example, it was common to blame homosexuals for the problems in the U.S.—even economic ones. Many conservative Christians would claim that God was punishing our country because of the sin of homosexuality.

This is clearly an unbiblical notion of theodicy but remains salient in fundamentalism, nonetheless. Let's again consider the story of Job. The story is predicated on the idea that Job was upright and righteous. He did nothing to deserve the evil that occurred. In fact, the idea of punishment theodicy was explicitly denounced in that story through the interventions of Jobs' friends.

Most attempts to address the problem of evil have been *defenses,* which are much weaker than theodicies. Theodicies attack the logical coherence of an argument; whereas defenses just provide reasons or excuses for why some idea is true. For example, a common defense might look like this: "Evil exists in the world because we are fallen creatures in need of redemption," or, "The Devil made me do it."

Perhaps the most famous defense for the problem of evil was performed by Augustine in what is known as "the free will defense." Augustine argued that there is evil in the world because humans have free will. Some will do good with that freedom and others will do evil. Twentieth century philosopher, Alvin Plantinga, would later re-articulate that argument by adding that evil is a *necessity* of free will. God did the greatest possible good by giving us that free will, even if it comes with the consequence of evil. This also means that God has already created the best possible world that we as humans can exist in.[12]

If we were to combine Augustine's free will defense with Leibniz's best possible world semantics and Plantinga's argument, we can re-articulate the free will defense as follows:[13]

1. The existence of evil is the result of a fallen human race attempting to live communally.

2. God's benevolence is exercised by providing humanity with free will.

3. Since God is all-knowing, powerful, and good, it must be the case that he has already created the best possible world where fallen humans can maintain their free will while, at the same time, living communally.

The key to his argument is that we currently live in the best possible world that could exist. The strength of this argument is its logical coherence. Also, it allows for the possibility of God to remain good while at the same time allowing evil to exist and humans to maintain their free will. This is a strong case for why evil exists and has been a favorite of religious philosophers for some time.

However, there are a couple of weaknesses with this argument. The first goes to the question of prayer. If God has already put into reality the best possible world, then prayer does not affect God to bring about change in the world. Therefore, prayer has no external value in this perspective because this is already the best possible outcome we could hope for. Any change to this world would be a place that was not as good as the current one.[14]

Secondly, although the free will argument addresses evil as it relates to humans, it doesn't address evil as it relates to creation. Why, for example, does the baby deer have to suffer through a forest fire? Why are their natural disasters? Questions like these are commonly addressed by arguing for humanity's influence over the creation as the consequence of our behavior toward it. However, the problem with this way of thinking is that natural disasters pre-date humanity. And, although I would agree that humanity has contributed to making things worse, it does not seem reasonable to think humans are the reason for natural suffering itself.

Outside of the fact that the problem of evil, as a whole, is conflated with presumptions, one could also take issue with the premise that somehow evil is a problem for the existence of God. The first issue I have with this presumption is that *evil has nothing to do with the existence of being*. If you take God out of the equation, there will still be evil. Ironically, God gives *meaning* to suffering because without him, suffering makes no sense. In fact, we might even argue that the existence of evil proves the existence of a being that is aware of our suffering and has already provided us with the best possible world to live in despite it. Evil in an atheistic universe is devoid of meaning because it cannot provide any meaningful explanation for its existence.

Therefore, how can someone worship a God who is supposedly all-powerful, yet allows humans to suffer? What's more, how does suffering convey love? My answer: because God could have done nothing. He could have let us spiral out of control into our own selfishness. He could have abandoned us. Not only does he not abandon us, but he also pursues us with zeal and unconditional love.

However, not only did he *not* abandon us, but he became a participant when he descended into the depths of humanity to wear our flesh. He did so to experience our injustice. He experienced the greatest type of pain in the sacrifice of his son. Our lord participated in this because his love runs to unfathomable depths. He suffered the greatest evil because he is just. God suffers as well. Perhaps he even suffers alongside us.

Humans suffer as a result of evil—sometimes directly, sometimes indirectly. We must create the necessary space within ourselves so that we might properly evolve into our suffering. If it is inevitable that we suffer, then we must do it well. If we want to love, then there is always the possibility of grief. It is human to grieve because it is human to love.

We cannot understand the depth of love the "father" has for his creation. Nevertheless, we will try to explore what that means in the next section.

The (F)ather: The Divine Will

The father (aka the Divine Will) is perhaps the most ignored person within the Trinity—even more than the Holy Spirit. One reason is that much of the information about him is subsumed into the life of Jesus or is conflated with "God." Jesus is the living Word, the one who reveals the father. The reason the father needs revealing is that he wasn't revealed beforehand. In Judaism, the "father" and "God" were identical because of Judaism's monotheism. In other words, the Jews did not know that when they addressed YAHWEH, they were addressing a triune God. Jesus doesn't just reveal the father, but his revelation is triune. That is, it points to all three persons of the Trinity.

The father is the first person of the Trinity. The title of "father" is one not based on the "maleness" of this being but is identified by Jesus as such because it is this person that Jesus proceeds *from* during the Incarnation. The "father/son" distinction is meant to illustrate this procession. However, we must be careful not to suggest that the title "father" refers to this person's "nature" instead of its "role". To believe that the father's title is reflective of its nature would require an acknowledgment that there is a hierarchical status between the two beings – one being more important or having greater authority than the other. This would violate the aforementioned trinitarian formula that we have been taking great care to preserve. Furthermore, the role of the persons of the Trinity is derivative of their function. This is how we know what their role is—it's deduced from their observed function.

The designation of "father" could also be a reference to Jesus's humanness. In other words, Jesus is the son of a human woman and a divine father. Therefore, he refers to him from which his earthly body came—just as he would refer to Mary as his mother.

The Divine Will is also the chief architect of the universe. It was his responsibility to Will into existence, through his Word, the collective universe.[15] It was his creative responsibility to create some "other" that could exist in relationship with himself. What's more, humans were fashioned in the image of God (*Imago Dei*). The human contains within its being the same beauty that God contains within itself. And the aspects of the triune God are captured in the human being. The human is a mind, which is willful, self-aware, and communicative.

From the depths of the dust, it was God's Will who churned over the dirt to fashion unto itself a being created in the likeness of God—the Divine Mind, and in the form of the Word, Jesus Christ. As a realistic expression of itself, God created humans to have purpose and meaning—to take control of their own destiny. They were fashioned to have the will to love—to receive it and to give it. They could choose to use this will for good or for evil—it would be their choice.

THERE ARE MANY EXPRESSIONS of the Trinity in our current context. The orthodox formula, that I have tried to maintain thus far, is not viewed as particularly relevant in today's context – though it's not entirely clear why. Any anti-modern approach to the Trinity will probably disregard any restrictions on its ability to express what it perceives to be an accurate delineation of God.

It is more important in modern contexts to try and show how God is reflected in the life of the believer and then move from there to some archetype.

Catholic theologian Elizabeth Johnson tackled this in her book, *Quest for the Living God*. Johnson asserts that this contemporary approach to understanding God is not only a modern approach but was the same method that the Early Church used to learn about God's nature. Johnson's book goes through and documents this approach throughout church history. Johnson believes that every generation that has considered the doctrine of the Trinity has begun with their experience of God and moved to the more abstract from there.

If this is true, it makes sense why those who tend to view God as a feminine deity, do so because it is the lens through which they experience God within their life. It is the same reason that theologians of the past (dominated largely by male thinking) have imagined God in masculine terms – and why this is so dominant in translations of the Bible. Ultimately, Johnson's view can be understood as the "inflection perspective" because it imagines how God inflects itself unto its creation. This means that there can be two seemingly contradicting perceptions of the Trinity that are both equally true based on how one experiences God (feminine, masculine, etc.).

This is a tough pill to swallow for many, especially if they view God in the absolute. It seems to create ontological confusion within the nature of God. God should be whatever it is in and of itself regardless of what we think or imagine it to be. In this chapter, I argued that God was neither male nor female because if it was one particular sex, then it would not have the experience of being the other and therefore lack something from how the image of God is shown in humans. We could say that God is both sexes, but that makes little sense. Therefore, God must transcend gender.

Humans are the closest analogy that exists to understand the nature of the Trinity. Internally, we exist in a similar way to the Trinity; we are minds in bodies; we have free will; we have self-awareness, and we have communicative discourse. We also exist externally (as the triune God does) in how we relate to one another and how we care for the well-being of the community around us. In other words, we are being most like our Creator when we are engaging with others in the world because that was how we were created to be.

DISCUSSION QUESTIONS

1. How do you see aspects of the Trinity expressed in your life and your relationship with others?

2. How do you think you would handle the Trinity issue if you lived during the Early Church?

3. What analogy would you use to describe the Trinity?

4. Do you think "eternal subordination" is a good analogy for the roles men and women have in relationships? Why or why not?

5. Do you think the "problem of evil" is a good argument against the existence of God? Why or why not?

4

JESUS: THE DIVINE WORD

"Jesus made possible not just a new way of understanding life,
but a new way of living it."
— ***Frederick Buechner***

"Jesus himself did not try to convert the two thieves on the cross;
he waited until one of them turned to him."
— ***Dietrich Bonhoeffer***

JESUS CHRIST IS THE most unique man to ever walk the Earth. He is the
beauty of God's truth lived out in a life that billions have tried to emulate for
more than two thousand years. Jesus wasn't unique because he claimed to be
divine; he was unique in how he used his divinity. Many people have claimed
to be divine throughout history.[1] Even in Jesus's time, people frequently
claimed to be the "promised one". However, only Jesus of Nazareth stuck
out in the cultural consciousness. Why is that? There was something about
Jesus that was different from the others. There was something that drew

people to him – all kinds of people. There was something about Jesus that persuaded his disciples not only to drop everything to follow him and record the ministry of his life but also to die for him. There was something so compelling about this man that a Pharisee named Saul was overwhelmed by a resurrected Jesus to the point where he not only followed him for the remainder of his life but also wrote what would become half of the New Testament.

No human did more to accomplish the Will of God than Jesus. God's Will expressed through Jesus demonstrated the extent to which God was willing to go for his creation. His love culminated in an act of reconciliation that humans had yearned for for thousands of years. Jesus fully restored a once broken relationship between humanity and God. Jesus is the self-expression of the Divine Will. You cannot know God's Will apart from encountering his Divine Word.[2]

Following Jesus does not mean that we become slaves to rules and regulations that lead to an ordinary life. Just the opposite. Following Jesus means that we become free to reinvent ourselves through the revelation of our true identities as beloved children of God. Through Jesus, we encounter what it really means to be human. Following Jesus requires a life of action – if we are not living a life of action, then we should evaluate whether we are really following Jesus.

Followers of Jesus become participants in building a kingdom of justice and equity. To become a follower of Jesus is to live greatly with purpose and security in an unjust, unsafe, and dark world. Following Jesus means that for the first time we truly live – even in death.

Perhaps the most important difference between progressive Christians and evangelicals is related to what is theologically *foundational* to each. For the evangelical, the Christological foundation is the atonement of Jesus,[3] whereby he is the ultimate sacrificial lamb for sin. For the progressive, the primary emphasis is on the love of Christ, both within his ministry, as well as his act upon the cross.

These differences are monumental, especially when they trickle down into other theological perspectives. When the foundation is different, all of the things that come after will also be different. This is why there is such a divide between progressive and evangelical theologies.

The Incarnation

Jesus, the eternal Word of God, came to the Earth and made himself flesh[4] as a servant for all of humanity.[5] Jesus came to put his full humanity on display as an example of how the individual should live their life before God and their neighbors.[6] His purpose was to do the will of the father.[7]

Many claim that Jesus was born of a virgin. This may sound unusual to 21st century readers but making claims about a virgin birth would not sound that strange to those in the first century. For example, the Phrygian-Roman god, Attis, was born of a virgin, Nana, on December 25. Attis would also go on to be resurrected after his death. Persephone was a virgin that gave birth twice without an earthly or heavenly father. There are plenty of additional ancient virgin birth stories. The fact that Jesus was born of a virgin is likely a myth that was later attributed to his birth. We cannot know that for sure. However, there is one argument that would demonstrate, at least in this one case, how it's possible that Jesus was born of a virgin. This is what I refer to as the "transmutation argument". We will discuss this more in the section below.

The Virgin Birth

The virgin birth is a core tenet of Christianity. Although the idea of a virgin birth was not uncommon during this time period, it does make our task of separating fact from fiction difficult, if not impossible.

Some have argued that there is a theological necessity for a virgin birth based on the uniqueness of Jesus (for example, his claim to be the son of

God). Some could even argue for genetics to be the reason why he should be born of a human by God. Although neither of these arguments is sufficient for providing theological justification for a virgin birth, they do point to an interesting question: How was the Divine Word transmuted into flesh from eternity?

The only way the entire Incarnation narrative makes sense with a virgin birth is by accepting the *transmutation argument*. This argument states that if it is true that Jesus was really related to God or was God in some way, there had to be a way for his eternal nature to transmute itself from its heavenly home to its earthly home. That transmutation would have to take place from one heavenly source to one earthly source. We get this in the virgin birth narrative.

Although this argument doesn't demonstrate proof in and of itself, it does demonstrate the necessity that exists if certain conditions are met (e.g., Jesus is eternal, Jesus is God, etc.). If the presuppositions are essentially true, then the argument is a valid continuation of those presuppositions. The problem is that you cannot validate the presuppositions; they are taken to be true on faith. However, this does demonstrate that holding faith in the virgin birth is at least logical.

For some reason, people are tempted to look for "earthly" explanations for miraculous events that are described in the Bible - as a way to explain away the miracles. No doubt much of the miraculous may have an earthly explanation, but this should not diminish their relevance. Perhaps some actual miracles have taken place – those with no earthly explanations. If Jesus was indeed who he said he was, then there does not need to be any additional explanation apart from the miraculous. The miraculous cannot be proven by empirical standards. Christians have *faith* in Jesus for this reason.

The virgin birth is one of those beliefs where faith seems completely un-reasonable for an individual to have. However, if we actually believe, in faith, that Jesus Christ was one-third of the Trinity, then a human being born of a virgin is not that far of a leap of faith. It is perhaps more reasonable to think that Mary had an affair and was attempting to hide it. It was for this reason that we might conclude that Mary did what any woman in the first century would do to save her reputation. However, the likelihood of the miraculous is fully contingent upon the fact that Jesus was who he said he was. With that said, I'm not sure how much it matters if Jesus was born of a virgin. Either reality would not make him any more or less divine.

The Nature of Jesus

The birth of Jesus by a woman represents his descent into being fully human. His descent from the father represents Jesus's divinity. His legitimate birth into humanity is important because it provides historicity for his existence. It is from this hypostatic union that classic Christianity asserts Jesus was fully human and fully divine.

Within this hypostatic union, Jesus adds the nature of humanity to his already divine nature. Upon the unification of these two natures, his human nature became eternal and exists even today where he resides "at the right hand" of the Divine Will.

Many evangelical theologians separate the nature of Jesus (or the person of Jesus) from his works. This should not be done. His work was infused with his nature. What he did never diverted from who he was. Therefore, we should view both his nature and works as one and the same.

For example, Jesus performed many miracles and preached often about social justice. This is not because Jesus happened to be an advocate for social reform. Instead, it is an insight into the nature of God. God is Just, and because of this, Jesus performed acts of justice during his time on Earth. One could argue that an extensive amount of justice was performed by Jesus throughout his ministry because justice is that important to God.

Equal Representation

The fact that Jesus was born a man and that he was born from a woman holds equal significance. One is not more important than the other.[8] Man and woman are equally represented in the Incarnation.

What does it mean that both men and women are equally represented? At least on a subconscious level, most theologians have elevated the power of men based upon the fact that Jesus came as a man—just as many Christians have done upon the basis that Adam was created first. Jesus did not become a man to make any statement specific to maleness, but rather to come into the Jewish tradition as a Rabbi. Jesus's treatment of men and women demonstrated that he valued both equally.

In fact, Jesus's treatment of women was counter-cultural for the time that he existed—not just within Judaism[9] but even in the Greco-Roman culture. One example of this are female disciples: Mary Magdalene, Susanna, Joanna, and many others.[10] Another is in how Jesus treated women—with care and compassion just as he did with men. For example, he referred to the woman with the bleeding disorder as a daughter of Abraham which gave her equality with the sons of Abraham.[11] His dealing with the woman who had committed adultery is also important to take note of because, given his status as a Rabbi, the woman should have been stoned according to the law. Not only did he protect her from death, but he showed kindness and compassion toward her. Perhaps the most distinct interaction came between Jesus and the Samaritan woman at the well. There exist so many cultural and religious taboos within that story that Jesus was certainly a social revolutionary. All of the barriers that the Jews established between men and women were broken down by Jesus. However, instead of following this example, people began building those walls back up again not long after he died.

The Divine Word as Revelation

There are many important doctrines and ideas related to Jesus, but the most important fundamental idea is the personal identity of Jesus. Who was Jesus Christ? Who did he claim to be? Who did others claim he was? Who did he think he was? These questions are of such importance that Christianity lives or dies depending on how they are answered.

It's important to understand that Jesus never specifically said he was God. He claimed to be a Rabbi[12] and, according to Matthew the tax collector, the father announced that Jesus was the son of God at Jesus's baptism.[13] Most importantly, Jesus was declared the Messiah by Peter and he accepted this title as being true.[14] To be the Messiah meant that he was the "promised one", the "savior" that the Hebrew people had been waiting for. We will dive deeper into what this means in the atonement section below.

An important note here about the use of the term, "son of God". The father calling Jesus the "son of God" and even Jesus's acceptance of this title was not related to the nature of his "maleness," nor is it saying anything about the nature of the "father". In fact, there is historical precedent that indicates why Jesus was called this. The Emperor of Rome during Jesus's ministry was Tiberius. Tiberius became known as *divi filius Augustus* or son of the God Augustus.[15] God used this popular idea to stand in contrast to the emperor of the time.

The most significant aspect of Jesus's nature is the fact that he was the Divine Revelation of God. It was Jesus's primary job to demonstrate what God was like and what it takes to accomplish God's will. John refers to Jesus as the eternal Word, "In the beginning was the Word, and the Word was with God, and the Word was God. He was with God in the beginning" (John 1:1). Moreover, when Christians say Jesus is the Divine Word, they are making an ontological claim - a claim made about the nature of something. This claim argued that Jesus's being could not be separated from his mission. In other words, Jesus's life was as much about what he *did* as it was about what he *said*.

Mid-to-late-20th century philosophy contributed some helpful linguistic categories to describe the connection between identity and action. Linguistic philosopher J.L. Austin, building upon Ludwig Wittgenstein, developed the idea of speech-acts as a linguistic framework for describing a specific type of reality, one where word and action are inseparable from one another. Jesus performing a speech-act means that there is no differentiation between what he said and what he did. Therefore, we can take confidence in the fact that the actions he performed were as authoritative as the content of his speech.

When we say that Jesus was a "speech-act" we are just using philosophical language to describe the theological concept of him being the Word of God. For Jesus to be the Word requires that he *reveals* and *acts* concurrently. He reveals the will of God, while also fulfilling what the will of God requires. Since the will of God requires action on behalf of the believer then Jesus is revealing the content (speech) through the works (actions) he performs.

This may sound unnecessarily complicated. However, understanding this idea is central to understanding the core reason for the Incarnation. If this point is not understood (as is often the case in evangelicalism), then we have missed the point of Jesus. In evangelicalism (and many other protestant movements), the person and works of Jesus are propositionalized and thus separated from their source. This problem was discussed in the section on The Problem of Systematic Theology earlier in this book. However, an example might prove to be useful. In systematic theology (the method most often employed by evangelicals) it becomes necessary in the analytic process to distinguish between the nature of Jesus and the works of Jesus. In other words, they separate belief from action in order to accommodate their methodology.

This might be understandable if we are talking about an ordinary human being. However, if we truly believe that Jesus is God, and the New Testament presumes this, then *who Jesus **is** cannot be separated from what Jesus **does**.* To do so would require making claims about Jesus that are untrue or leaving out important aspects of who he was for methodological purposes.

Jesus as the Divine Word came not on his own authority, but on that of the Divine Will so that God could break into time, into history, to express his love towards his creation. Swiss Catholic theologian Hans Urs Von Balthasar states:

> "... the son can do nothing of himself. He cannot speak on his own authority. And so, he does not do his own will, although he has a will of his own...but he is always what he is on the basis of 'not my own will'."[16]

The Incarnation of the Divine Word required that Jesus's personal identity (in the human sense) collapsed into the Divine Will so that when he proclaimed, "I am he,"[17] he was, in fact, revealing the Divine Will. This is none the more evident in the scene when Jesus speaks to Peter about his nature in Matthew 6:16-17.

> When Jesus came to the region of Caesarea Philippi, he asked his disciples, "Who do people say the Son of Man is?" They replied, "Some say John the Baptist; others say Elijah; and still others, Jeremiah or one of the prophets." "But what about you?" he asked. "Who do you say I am?" Simon Peter answered, "You are the Messiah, the Son of the living God." Jesus replied, "Blessed are you, Simon son of Jonah, for this was not revealed to you by flesh and blood, but by my Father in heaven."

This was previously discussed in Chapter 2, but a brief mention here about the nature of the Bible as a means of revelation is necessary. Theologians often refer to the Bible as the special revelation that God gives to humans for them to know him better. This is true, in so far as it provides information about God that we could otherwise not know. However, it is more accurate to understand the Bible as a way to access the revelation that has been displayed by God and through the life of Jesus Christ.[18] This is why both the Hebrew Scriptures and the New Testament are "testaments". *They are testimonies to the revelation that occurred at certain points in history.* I believe this is an important distinction to make. However, theologians often argue that in order for Jesus to be the true revelation of God, he must be sinless; otherwise, he could not be the son of God.

Was Jesus Perfect or Sinless?

Impeccability is the fancy theological term for the perfection of Jesus. The question that arises here is whether or not being perfect and being sinless are exactly the same thing. Most evangelicals will not make this distinction. However, the only way the two are synonymous is if "sin" is viewed as an ethical mandate. In the Hebrew Scriptures, a sinner is understood to be someone who does not follow the law. This understanding is incorrect. The New Testament clarifies the meaning by describing sin as disobedience to the will of God. Although following the will of God might also be ethical at times, it is not *necessary* for it to be in order to be the will of God.

Jesus's goal was not ethical perfection; his goal was sinlessness.[19] If one views sin and perfection synonymously, then Jesus *must be* ethically perfect in order to be sinless, but this requirement is not needed. This is a vital distinction to make because Christians spend an unnecessary amount of time worrying about their own ethical perfection when they should be worried about fulfilling the will of God (which may or may not include an ethical mandate.) God never demanded ethical perfection of humans, so why do so many churches focus on this and not doing the will of God?

Total Depravity

As an aside, there is a tangential, yet important discussion regarding the doctrine of total depravity. I believe there is an argument to be made against this doctrine - which asserts that all people are born into a sinful nature by simply being born. And yet, somehow Jesus was not born with this nature. It is often argued that the reason for this is that he did not have an earthly father. If it is true that Jesus was born without total depravity, then it is logical to conclude that it must be transferred through either sex or more specifically, sperm – which is a ridiculous idea. So why would Jesus be born without total depravity and other humans are? Given this question, we are left with only two possible answers. Either Jesus *was* born with total depravity, or no one is.

However, since those who hold to total depravity also argue that sex is good within the confines of marriage (between a man and a woman), then it doesn't hold true that sex is the primary means of total depravity transmission, which is what appears to be the central argument. Furthermore, God tells Adam and Eve to "be fruitful and multiply" in Genesis 1:22—before the Fall when sin entered the world. If sex were a sin, it would mean procreating is a sin. In other words, under this argument for humans to live in obedience to God, we would have to stop procreating, but would go directly against the expressed will of God. I believe this puts to rest any claim that total depravity—at least in its traditional form—can cause the transmission of sin into humans simply because they are born.

Although Scripture and tradition testify to the impeccability of Jesus, the question we are left with is "does it matter if Jesus was perfect or sinless?" The only context in which it would matter is if Jesus is atonement for our sin (as penal substitution argues). There doesn't seem to be an obvious relationship between his righteousness and his impeccability, which would mean that his death can still be a sacrifice to accomplish reconciliation even if he was not perfect.

When we make "ethical perfection" a primary focus of Jesus's life, we ignore the other important virtues of his life. The fact that nothing in the Gospels emphasize ethical perfection, this leads me to believe that Jesus's impeccability is irrelevant – especially in light of the other works he performed. His other works were solely focused on re-establishing relationships between humanity and God. In other words, his works were about reconciliation and not about ethics.

This necessitates that we discuss the doctrine of atonement so that we can understand the primary work of the cross. The next section will address the atonement question and assess how relevant it is and whether our traditional view of the atonement of Jesus (penal substitution) is an appropriate perspective on one of Jesus's most important acts.

Atonement

The doctrine of atonement is arguably the most important doctrine to venture through. Understanding the reason why Jesus went to the cross colors how we see his entire life. Various atonement theories have been used throughout Church history. Penal Substitution Atonement Theory (PSA) is the most popular and the most recognizable. However, it is important to note that other theories also exist. These theories are summarized in the table below.

Atonement Theory	Influence	Description
Christus Victor	Irenaeus	Jesus died in order to defeat the powers of evil and free mankind from their bondage.
Ransom	Origen	Jesus died as a ransom sacrafice - a payment that was owed either to the father or Satan.
Moral Influence	Augustine	Jesus died to bring about some positive change in the world.
Satisfaction	Anselm	Jesus died to mend what was broken and satisfy God's requirement for Justice.
Penal Substitution	The Reformation	Jesus died as a sacrafice to appease the wrath of God over sin.
Governmental	Methodism	Jesus suffered punishment for our sin and propitiates God's wrath.
Scapegoat	Rene Girard	Jesus died as a scapegoat for humanity. He is not sacraficed as much as he is a victim of being human.

Penal Substitution Atonement Theory (PSA)

PSA asserts that Jesus was punished (penalized) in our place (substitution) for sin. This is viewed as necessary because the Divine Will's wrath must be in some way quenched to appease God's holiness. This is the classic evangelical perspective on the nature of Christ's sacrifice for humanity. What PSA Theory fails to do is explain how God's love can be reconciled with his wrath. In other words, how can God have such wrath for a creation that he loves, while at the same time, not having at least the same amount of love for the only begotten son, Jesus? This type of love should spare Jesus of that wrath, right? PSA Theory also fails to explain why there is a need for a sacrifice to begin with. God didn't require sacrifice in the Hebrew Scriptures, as many of us have been taught, so why all of a sudden would he require it in the New Testament?

Then there is the question of justice. This is similar to the question of love. If it is true that forgiveness requires justice, then where is the justice for Jesus? In fact, one could argue that his murder was the greatest injustice in history. This begs the question, "How can one injustice create a moment of justice for another?" These are difficult, if not impossible, questions for the PSA advocate to answer.

Below is the narrative that evangelical Christianity asserts in the context of PSA. This narrative will bring together many of the doctrines we have discussed thus far.

1. All humans are sinners, born into sin because of the Fall of Adam and Eve. This is referred to as total depravity.

2. No human can provide the sacrifice needed to atone for their depravity.

3. God provided the perfect, unblemished sacrifice for our sins—Jesus Christ.

4. Jesus lived a perfect, sinless life.

5. God required that Jesus be sacrificed upon the cross to pay the *penalty* for our sins.

6. For us to receive forgiveness for our sins, we need to ask Jesus to be our personal *savior*. (In other words, accept this narrative as true.)

Despite what evangelicals may tell you, penal substitution does not have historical roots in the Early Church and is, therefore, not orthodox. Penal substitution theology came out of the Reformation (in the 1500s) and specifically from two men named Martin Luther (who started its formation) and John Calvin (who was educated as a lawyer). Calvin used his legal training as a framework for how to understand the sacrifice of Christ. What this means is that no one believed in the idea that Jesus paid the penalty for our sins for the first 1,500 years of Christianity. Of course, this does not make the doctrine wrong, but it certainly is not orthodox.

The main problem with PSA is that it is based on the premise that God requires a sacrifice for sin as illustrated through the sacrificial system in the Hebrew Scriptures. However, God never told Israel that they needed to participate in any sacrificial system. It is either an assumption the Jews made, or it was a way for the priests to enforce Jewish law. For certain, Jewish laws were extrapolations of the commands God gave to Moses.

> For in the day that I brought them out of the land of Egypt,
> I did not speak to your fathers or command them concerning
> burnt offerings and sacrifices. But this command I gave them:
> "Obey my voice, and I will be your God, and you shall be my
> people. And walk in all the way that I command you, that it
> may be well with you." (Jeremiah 7:22-23, ESV)[20]

Atonement for sin is not the logical conclusion one draws from the Hebrew Scriptures. It's adherence to the will of God – the same thing that the Gospels proclaim was the purpose of Jesus. Furthermore, Jesus never said he came to sacrifice for sin, but rather to do the will of the father. In John 6:38 Jesus says, "For I have come down from heaven, not to do my own will but the will of him who sent me" (ESV). The same thing can be read in John 5:30 as well, "I can do nothing on my own. As I hear, I judge, and my judgment is just because I seek not my own will but the will of him who sent me" (ESV).

If the explicit purpose of Jesus was never to atone for sin, then what was that purpose? The only way to answer this question is to understand what happened in the Garden of Eden because Jesus came to fix whatever occurred there.

Traditionally evangelical theology takes the atonement of Jesus and imports that into the story of Adam and Eve; instead of allowing the Genesis story to speak organically. However, if we read the text non-anachronistically, we see something different emerge. Genesis 3's emphasis is not on the sin that was committed, but on the fact that Adam and Eve did not listen to God. They did not obey his will.

The biblical narrative tells a different story when it comes to the purpose of the Incarnation. Focusing on disobedience to the will of God creates a logical extension from the Hebrew Scriptures to the New Testament when Jesus says he came to do the "will of the Father". Jesus had to accomplish what Adam and Eve could not. This grants Jesus the title of "the second Adam".[21] Jesus came to listen so that he could know and accomplish God's will. This is echoed in the aforementioned Jeremiah passage when he says "...obey my voice, and I will be your God, and you shall be my people . . ."

The same theme can be seen throughout the Hebrew Scriptures. For example, the primary purpose of the Ten Commandments was not the conviction of sin. Its purpose was to guide Israel despite its sin. All Israel needed to do was what God commanded them. Instead of just obeying the given commandments, the religious leaders parsed the commandments out into hundreds of laws for Israel to follow. What's more, the Israelites also created a sacrificial system to atone for when there was disobedience to the law. However, as Hosea 6:6 reminds us, none of this was what God asked them to do. "For I desire steadfast love and *not sacrifice*, the knowledge of God *rather than burnt offerings,*" (ESV).

We also see the theme of obedience/disobedience in the Prophets and how they were treated by Israel. The role of the prophet was to speak on behalf of God, to communicate God's will to the people. All the Israelites had to do was listen to them. Some did, but most did not. Again, we are confronted with the theme of listening and obeying God's will.

If God did not require sacrifice in the Old Testament, then he didn't require it in the New Testament. If it is true that Jesus came to listen, reveal, and obey the Will of God, then everything we read about Jesus changes.

What then was the purpose of the Incarnation? Author Keith Giles summarizes this nicely:

The offering of the body of Jesus is not a picture of Jesus being sacrificed to appease God's wrath or fulfill God's Justice. Instead, it is a picture of Christ's obedience to the will of God.[22]

The Apostle Paul perfectly summarizes the purpose of Christ in 2 Corinthians 5:17-21:

Therefore, if anyone is in Christ, the new creation has come: The old has gone, the new is here! All this is from God, who reconciled us to himself through Christ and gave us the ministry of reconciliation: that God was reconciling the world to himself in Christ, not counting people's sins against them. And he has committed to us the message of reconciliation. We are therefore Christ's ambassadors, as though God were making his appeal through us. We implore you on Christ's behalf: Be reconciled to God. God made him who had no sin to be sin for us, so that in him we might become the righteousness of God.

What Do We Do About Sin?

What then are we to do about all of the passages that talk about Jesus dying for sin? This story is so ingrained in our subconscious it seems axiomatic to assume that Jesus died for our sins. What is needed to properly understand these passages is a shift of perspective. Consider that Jesus did not die *for* our sins, instead he died *because* of our sins. It was not the will of God to sacrifice Jesus for mankind's sin. Instead, it was God's will that Jesus demonstrates what it means to live as a human being and that included death. As Paul reminds us in 2 Corinthians 5:21, "God made him who had no sin to be sin for us, so that in him we might become the righteousness of God."

Again, Keith Giles eloquently puts it this way:

> ... so, it's not so much that Christ died for us as it is that Christ died as us – in union with us and with the Father and the Spirit – and that in his dying all died, and in his rising, all were raised into newness of life with Christ.[23]

Just as the Word and the Will are one in the Divine sense, so too is Jesus one with humanity in the human sense. Jesus enfleshed himself in humanity through the Incarnation. He empathized with humanity through his death. He reconciled humanity through his resurrection. Jesus became, and remains forever, connected with humanity. This connection was necessary to *reconcile* what first happened in the Garden of Eden. Jesus became the second Adam[24] and in so doing lived as a human being and demonstrated the possibility for humans to live in the Will of God. But, unlike Adam, Jesus conquered death. Unlike Adam, Jesus conquered life.

Now that we understand Jesus's purpose from this perspective, I would like to now argue, somewhat paradoxically, that Jesus did save us from our sins. He saved us in the sense that sin is a by-product of our disobedience to will of God. God saved us from our sin, by providing the example of obeying the will of God in life and death. But Jesus did not save us from our depravity – he did not save us from some ethical inadequacy.

The Resurrection

The resurrection is the final act of Jesus's earthly life. Therefore, it is of the utmost importance that we take a moment to understand the purpose of the resurrection and think about whether it is something that has veracity to it.

Many, if not most progressives, will deny the miracles of Jesus if there is a more reasonable earthly explanation for their efficacy. Perhaps the most impressive miracle recorded in the Bible is the resurrection of Jesus after being dead in a tomb for three days. One of the most prevalent earthly explanations for the resurrection is that the disciples lied about the event to save face. Perhaps this is a later addition to the story to add creditably to the Jesus narrative, which was a common practice of the time among those who claimed individuals had God-like characteristics. As a result of this, many progressives fall into one of these two perspectives.

Although many progressives will say they think it is unreasonable to believe in a literal resurrection, I would like to argue for a more orthodox version that maintains a belief in the resurrection. I would find it difficult to be a Christian without believing in the resurrection because it would make the life of Christ irrelevant. If he did die and never rose, then he was not who he said he was.

I would like to put forth two simple reasons why I still believe in a literal resurrection. First, if it was true that the story of the resurrection was made up, then the disciples would know and yet, most of them died a martyr's death for a cause they would have known to be false. This makes little sense. Their deaths as martyrs demonstrate to what extent they believed that Jesus had risen from the dead. They were willing to die for that belief.

Second, I think that if Jesus was "from God", then the resurrection is the only thing that could make sense. It is hard for me to rationalize a story where God became incarnate and then died—and that was it. Jesus wouldn't be much of a God. That means if someone is going to deny the resurrection, then they have to deny the deity of Jesus. That is a leap some are not willing to make—including me.

Although the resurrection and subsequent ascension are the final acts of Jesus's earthly life, I would argue that his return, whatever that looks like, is the final act of his story. It is the final act of the metanarrative that has been taking shape for millennia. Even though much of what can be known about the return of Jesus is limited, if not completely null, it is still important to understand why many evangelicals hold to this belief.

End Times

For many, the resurrection and subsequent ascension provide a foundation for the return of Jesus Christ. Acts 1:11 provides evidence for this hope.

> "Men of Galilee," they said, "why do you stand here looking into the sky? This same Jesus, who has been taken from you into heaven, will come back in the same way you have seen him go into heaven."

Few things are debated in theological circles as much as eschatology (the study of the end times). In fact, it is so important that there are even denominations and independent churches that have formed with eschatology as their primary theological locus. Those who study the end times from a Christian perspective are primarily concerned with answering two questions: First, when will the rapture occur? Second, when will Christ return?

Debates surrounding the end times are primed for propositionalists. It is one of those areas of study that almost begs for proof-texting since it requires the systematic organization of prophetic ideas. Some theologians attempt to decode the prophetic works of Scripture to predict dates when certain end times events will occur. The Book of Revelation documents many of these events, although some are spread throughout the Hebrew Scriptures as well. I will not spend much time on this section because much of the end times debate is spent on things that we really cannot know.[25] However, a brief explanation of the doctrine might prove useful for some.

Many Christians believe in the rapture - an event where all who believe in Christ will be taken up to Heaven in the "twinkling of an eye".[26] Believers in the rapture usually speculate on when this event will occur. Will it be before (pre-tribulation rapture), in the middle of (mid-tribulation rapture), or after (post-tribulation rapture) a "tribulation period"? Many Christians understand the tribulation period as a time lasting seven years divided into two parts. The first three-and-a-half years is a peaceful time, and the second three-and-a-half years is when God empties his wrath upon the Earth. However, where there is more debate is whether Christians will have to go through this period or not.

A second and primary issue related to the end times is when Christ will return to establish the new kingdom. For those who hold this belief, most agree that it will be after the rapture. The debate on Christ's return is closely linked to the Millennium mentioned in the Book of Revelation. According to Revelation 20, the Millennium is a period of 1,000 years where there will be peace on Earth. Will Jesus be the one that ushers in that peace as "premillennialism" argues, or will he return after that time of peace as "postmillennialism" argues? There is also a minority third view which is referred to as "Amillennialism". This group doesn't believe there will be any millennium period. All of this speculation is based upon a certain way of reading Revelation 20. How certain events line up in one's eschatology determines the type of millennialist they are.

This is somewhat of an overly simplistic survey of eschatology, but very little, if any "truth", can really be known about this area of study. Theologians have claimed the end is near for as long as people have thought about these things. Instead of existing in a state of waiting for an apocalyptic event to occur, we should instead be more focused on what is happening in our world now.

What is the Gospel?

The New Testament contains many references to "preaching the Gospel" or "preaching the good news". We find this in the Gospels themselves and the writings of the apostles. It is of the utmost importance to understand the content of the Gospel because it tells the story of Jesus. The Gospel is the thing that makes Christians, "Christian." When Jesus said, "believe in me,"[27] he was saying "believe in the Gospel".

Since I've already argued that atonement is not central to the Gospel story, there must be something else to replace it. Luke 9:1-3 provides some insight.

> When Jesus had called the Twelve together, he gave them pow-
> er and authority to drive out all demons and to cure diseases,
> and he sent them out to *proclaim the kingdom of God and to
> heal the sick.* He told them: "Take nothing for the journey—no
> staff, no bag, no bread, no money, no extra shirt." (emphasis
> mine)

Jesus sent out the disciples to proclaim the Kingdom of God, long before there was any discussion of atonement. Not only does this mean that the Gospel is not primarily about atonement (as much of evangelicalism's rendition of the Gospel is), but it also means that the primary tenants of the message are social.

> Jesus went throughout Galilee, teaching in their synagogues,
> proclaiming the good news of the kingdom, and healing every
> disease and sickness among the people. News about him
> spread all over Syria, and people brought to him all who were
> ill with various diseases, those suffering severe pain, the de-
> mon-possessed, those having seizures, and the paralyzed; and
> he healed them. (Matthew 4:22-24)

These two passages (and the many others like them) help construct a different Gospel story than the one many of us were taught. Jesus came to establish the Kingdom of God. This is the Gospel, the good news, and what ought to be preached as the central message of Christianity. The actions that this Gospel should lead to are acts of social justice in the name of Christ (heal the sick, cure diseases, feed the hungry, etc.). This is what we are told the Kingdom of God is to look like.

It can be hard to strive for something, like the Kingdom of God, if we don't understand what it is. The New Testament is not entirely clear as to what the Kingdom of God looks like. It is defined in several different ways from a spiritual place (Heaven) to a physical place on Earth. The best indication we have is by the life that Jesus lived because he lived a life shaped by the Kingdom. If we are to live like him then we are to do God's will. If we are doing God's will, then we are participating in the building of this kingdom.

Traditional evangelicalism typically understands the kingdom as people becoming "saved", that Christians are "building the kingdom" when souls are coming to Christ. But this is, at best, a very small part of the story and, at worst, completely incorrect. Where this idea comes from is not entirely clear, but it is not biblical. Building the kingdom is not *adding* one thing to another (adding new souls), Instead, it is *transforming* one thing *into* another. If people becoming part of the Church is how that transformation occurs, then great. However, that cannot be the only or even the primary way of building the Kingdom of God. It is one of the reasons why many Christians need deconstruction. It is why they need better spiritual management.

The healings in the New Testament are taken literally by most Christians. I don't know if anyone, other than Jesus, can perform a miracle like healing someone simply by speaking it into existence. I do know that many people can feed the poor. Many can help find homes for the homeless. Many can welcome foreigners and help the elderly. Jesus went to where the need was. He did not simply wait for the need to come to him. Perhaps we need to consider expanding our expectations when it comes to what it means to proclaim the good news. The only way to accomplish this is to observe how Jesus interacted with those within his culture and do accordingly in ours.

Jesus and Culture

An overarching yet tangential question to consider is, "What is Jesus's relationship to culture? How has he been imagined, reimagined, and understood within the Western culture?" The answer to this question has monumental consequences as it determines how Christians understand their mission within the culture.

H. Richard Niebuhr is best known for his work, "Christ and Culture", where he explores this very question. Niebuhr posited that Christ's relationship to culture has taken various forms throughout history. His triadic observation is:

Christ *against* culture – Represented in the monastic tradition, as well as Tertullian's works, it asserts that Christ is in opposition to culture and, as such, Christians should reject it.

Christ *of* culture – The one who comes to save and remake culture.

Christ *above* culture – The fundamental issue is not with God and culture, but with God and humanity.

Niebuhr suggests that Christians should not choose one perspective at the exclusion of the others, but instead understand all three as potentially applicable at any given time. He does not go on to illustrate what this looks like, but his primary concern is with the ever-changing nature of culture. The idea is that each role or version of Jesus has its own place within society depending on society's opinion or practice of Jesus at that time.

Although all three are problematic independently, there may be merit to understanding them in conjunction with each other. The application of each one is not due to the nature of that particular culture (as Niebuhr suggests). Instead, we should synthesize all three to work together at the same time, regardless of how the culture sees Jesus at that time.

For example, when culture is against Jesus Christians often remain solely in a state of *Christ against culture,* asserting that they must stand with Christ against the culture. However, this Christ is also the Christ of grace, and therefore, once a culture observes their need for the *Christ of culture,* they accept his grace. At the same time, *Christ is above culture.* Christ is God and should be worshiped as such. With this synthesized understanding, Christ is concurrently transcendent (far) and imminent (near) to culture.

Jesus: The Social Crusader

Jesus was one of the most revolutionary social crusaders in human history. His commitment to social justice is evident throughout the pages of the New Testament. Despite this, there is much stigma around social justice in the U.S. today. Social justice is often viewed as a left-wing political ideology that is indicative of the "bleeding heart liberal". It's not altogether clear when advocating for social justice became the responsibility of left-leaning Christians. The Gospel not only teaches us that this was Jesus's mission, but his life illustrated it.

There are many social issues that one can be involved in that are just as glorifying to God as Jesus's spectacular miracles. In fact, Jesus tells us that if we believe in him, we will do even greater things.[28]

We have to stop limiting our actions related to social justice based upon our political preferences. Instead, we should let our social convictions dictate those preferences. Jesus needs to stop taking a back seat to political ideology.

It was only the injustice of the cross that could restore justice to the world. Followers of Christ should be catalysts for change, actively loving and helping those in need; this was the calling for the early followers and it remains our call still today. We talked a lot in this chapter about how the Incarnation was about following the will of God. This is more than just poetic symbolism. The Incarnation was a real event. Jesus was a real person whose purpose was to restore justice within Israel and to bring Gentiles into the fold.[29]

JESUS MEANS MANY THINGS to many people. How Jesus is expressed in the world differs depending on the individual making him manifest. To some, Jesus is the full expression of love demonstrated in the world. To others, he is the foundation for all revealed truth. Regardless of how we live him out in the world, we are united under a common banner. Regardless of a person's opinion on the divinity of Jesus, his message was simple. When asked by the religious leaders, "What is the greatest commandment?" Jesus responded thusly:

> Love the Lord your God with all your heart and with all your soul and with all your mind.' This is the first and greatest commandment. And the second is like it: "Love your neighbor as yourself." All the Law and the Prophets hang on these two commandments. (Matthew 22:36-40)

Christians often emphasize one (loving God) to the exclusion of the other (loving neighbors). Christians need to understand that the call to do the will of God and to love those around us must be fully embraced to reflect the example Jesus displayed and represent him to the fullest at all times.

Discipleship in the Church should make the life of Jesus its ultimate priority. Not just learning information about what he did but practicing those works in the real world. James 2:14-26 tells us that a life lived like Christ demonstrates our faith to the world. You cannot claim to be a person of faith if Christ is not evidenced by your faith. In fact, it is not possible to just believe in Jesus because those who believe in him necessarily do what he does because they know that is what belief requires.

DISCUSSION QUESTIONS

1. How would you describe who Jesus Christ is?

2. Do you think Jesus was born of a virgin? How much do you think it matters?

3. Do you think Jesus was sinless? Do you think there is a difference between his sinlessness and his perfection? If so, what are those differences?

4. Do you hold to an Atonement or Reconciliation Theory? If Atonement, which version do you think is more likely?

5. Do you believe that Jesus will return? Do you fall into any of the theological perspectives listed above? If so which one and why?

6. When Jesus was incarnated on earth was he then absent in heaven, or did he co-exist in both?

5

THE HOLY SPIRIT: DIVINE CONSCIOUSNESS

"Jesus taught us to pray, 'Forgive us our trespasses as we forgive those who trespass against us,' not forgive us and smite those bastards who hurt us."
—Nadia Bolz-Weber

"Prayer is not what is done by us, but rather what is done by the Holy Spirit in us."
—Henri Nouwen

IN THEOLOGICAL CIRCLES, THE study of the Holy Spirit is referred to as Pneumatology. The Holy Spirit is one of the least studied doctrines in Christianity despite the fact that the Holy Spirit is the most active member of the Trinity within the believer's life. It is not just evangelicalism that has largely downplayed the role of the Holy Spirit. Most theologians take little time to try to understand this nebulous figure – with the notable exception of charismatic/Pentecostal theologians.

The primary reason for this lack of theological attention is that the role the Spirit plays in Scripture can be unclear. As a result, theologians often find it difficult to be both comprehensive and accurate in their treatment of the Spirit. Perhaps the most comprehensive treatment was done by evangelical Graham Cole in his work, "He Who Gives Life: The Doctrine of the Holy Spirit".[1] The nature of the Holy Spirit's relationship to the Trinity, the Church, and humanity is of utmost importance for Christians to understand and it can only serve to deepen one's appreciation for this divine member of the Trinity. After all, the Spirit is responsible for the entirety of the believer's spiritual life.

Third Person of the Trinity

If Jesus is the Divine Word and the father is the Divine Will, what then is the Holy Spirit? I refer to the third person of the Trinity as the Divine Consciousness. This Consciousness is the final necessary component within the Trinity because it links the other two persons of the Trinity to the Divine Mind. (It is also what links believers to the Divine Mind.) The Divine Consciousness is a logical necessity if we believe that the Trinity is self-aware – something that is not possible apart from consciousness. Consciousness is the last component necessary to complete the Divine Mind.

The primary aspect which elevates humans over animals is a sense of self. It is the chief attribute of the mind. Self-awareness not only allows humans to form a personal identity, but it helps the individual understand their psychological horizon in conjunction with the world around them. In other words, self-awareness helps individuals understand their place in the world. It also allows the individual to differentiate their place in the world from others who are like them. We will discuss this concept more in the section on personal identity in the next chapter.

These same attributes are true in the Divine Mind as well. Since humans are created in the image of God, then it is reasonable to believe that such an important aspect of our minds would be just as present in the Divine Mind it was imagined from.

The foremost question to consider about the Holy Spirit is not related to its role within the Trinity but rather whether it should even be given Divine status. Let's consider whether the Spirit described in the Bible is one person within the Trinity or simply an attribute of God. There are many attributes of God described in the Bible, for example, Holiness and Power. Why does God's "Spirit" get special status as a member of the Trinity?

First, the Divine Consciousness is *personal*. In Romans 8:26, Paul describes this personality, "In the same way, the Spirit helps us in our weakness. We do not know what we ought to pray for, but the Spirit himself intercedes for us through wordless groans." In other words, the Divine Consciousness is intimately connected to our lives in such a way that it knows how to intercede for us in times where we are unable to do it ourselves.

Second, the Divine Consciousness is *active*. It is active not only throughout the Hebrew Scriptures but is also the Power by which Jesus performed his miracles. Many historical sources explicitly talk about the Spirit – both biblical and extrabiblical. The Holy Spirit's first appearance in the biblical narrative was as an active participant in the creation story.

Third, the fact that the Spirit also participated in the creation means that it is also *Divine*. Its divinity and activity can be seen in Genesis 1:1–2:

> In the beginning God created the heavens and the earth. Now the earth was formless and empty, darkness was over the surface of the deep, and the *Spirit of God* was hovering over the waters. (emphasis mine)

The personal, active, and Divine status of the Divine Consciousness are seen working together in 2 Samuel 23:2: "The Spirit of the Lord spoke

through me; his word was on my tongue." This passage demonstrates all
of the different aforementioned attributes that the Divine Consciousness
possesses in a single passage. Passages like this can be seen throughout the
Hebrew Scriptures (e.g., Ezekiel 36:27; Psalm 143:10; Isaiah 11:12).

It is also the Divine Consciousness who is the object of adoration for the
nation of Israel within the Temple.[2] Just as the Spirit was present in the
Jewish temple, so too is it equally present within the believer. The body is a
temple[3] for the Divine Consciousness and must be cared for and maintained
just as one would for a physical temple. Paul affirms this in 1 Corinthians
6:19, "Do you not know that your bodies are temples of the Holy Spirit, who
is in you, whom you have received from God?"

The presence of the Divine Consciousness was described differently in the
Hebrew Scriptures than it was in the New Testament and as it is today. In the
Jewish tradition, the Divine Consciousness was not always present within the
Jewish believer as it is the Christian today. Instead, the Divine Consciousness
was invoked through various types of worship and prayer. The indwelling of
the Divine Consciousness was special and only occurred for someone like a
prophet. There was not a constant indwelling like what Jesus testifies to in
the New Testament. This is demonstrated in the prophetic writing of Isaiah
61:1 - which interestingly, is also the passage that Jesus preached for his first
message to the world in Luke 4.

> The Spirit of the Sovereign Lord is on me because
> the Lord has anointed me to proclaim good news to the poor.
> He has sent me to bind up the brokenhearted, to proclaim
> freedom for the captives and release from darkness for the
> prisoners . . ."

In fact, one could argue that the Divine Consciousness was the primary
person of the Divine Trinity present within the Hebrew Scriptures. This
Divine Consciousness was involved in communicating prophecy—in word,

through dreams, and in visions. The Divine Consciousness is also granted inclusion into the Trinity by Jesus in what is formally known as the "Great Commission."[4]

> Therefore, go and make disciples of all nations, baptizing them in the name of the Father and of the Son and of the *Holy Spirit*, and teaching them to obey everything I have commanded you" (Matthew 28:19-20, emphasis mine).

The Early Church used the Matthew 28 formula for their baptismal creeds. Those creeds serve as the first indication we have that the Church Fathers included the Trinity within their ecclesiastical practice.

Attributes

The Divine Consciousness is most often imagined as wind or breath (*Ruach*). It is an invisible force that has the ability to be felt, but not seen. It is often manifested as the power of God throughout the Old Testament and is seen as the "helper" in the New Testament.[5]

The Divine Consciousness is most often associated with "spiritual gifted-ness." That is, those gifts or special skills that are given to Christians upon conversion to help bolster the Church's mission. However, there is so much more to the Divine Consciousness than its ability to impart special skills that can be used by the Church.

The Divine Consciousness is also a Spirit of wisdom. Through indwelling, its purpose is to convict and apply biblical/spiritual wisdom to the believer. Here "wisdom" is understood as the ability to accurately integrate biblical/spiritual knowledge into a lived experience in the real world.

The Divine Consciousness is also our *paraclete* (advocate).[6] It teaches Christians in ways that non-Christians don't have the opportunity to experience. It is responsible for transforming the Scriptures into the Word of God for the believer. Ultimately it offers Christians support, strength, and counsel and intercedes for Christians when necessary.[7]

The only way to truly appreciate the Divine Consciousness' role in the believer's life is to understand where it came from and why it appeared. At the Passover recounted in John 14, Jesus tells his disciples that he will be leaving soon, but he will leave for them a Helper so that they will not be alone. This promise is not just for the disciples but extends to all believers. This promised One was delivered to the Christian faithful during an event called Pentecost.

Pentecost and its Legacy

Pentecost was a Divine event recorded in Acts 2 which took place during the Jewish holiday of thanksgiving for first fruits called "The Feast of Weeks" or *"Shavuot"*. This event was a great way for the Divine Consciousness to make itself known in a significant way since there were pilgrims from all over attending the festival, pilgrims who spoke various languages and dialects.

When the day of Pentecost came, they were all together in one place. Suddenly a sound like the blowing of a violent wind came from heaven and filled the whole house where they were sitting. They saw what seemed to be tongues of fire that separated and came to rest on each of them. All of them were filled with the Holy Spirit and began to speak in other tongues as the Spirit enabled them" (Acts 2:1-4).

The story goes on to say that Peter stood before the large group of pilgrims and preached the Gospel. He explained to the group what was happening and how they had the ability to speak in other languages. He concluded by explaining to the group what happened to Jesus, that he was crucified, died, and was raised back to life. In other words, Jesus was the one promised beforehand.

This is the first time in Scripture that the practice of "speaking in tongues" is mentioned. Whether or not this practice continued beyond Pentecost is not as clear, although many Christians within Pentecostal faith traditions claim to practice it regularly. We do know that the Corinthian church practiced speaking in tongues,[8] but whether this was widespread or whether it continued into the Patristic Father's generation is not proven.

There are two historical references to speaking in tongues worth mentioning. In the 4th century, both Irenaeus[9] and Tertullian[10] briefly mention events where people were speaking in unknown languages.[11] However, not much detail is given as to the circumstances or to the extent that this was practiced.

Speaking in tongues has been practiced in the church in one of two ways. First, there is the version displayed in Acts, where the practitioner spoke a natural language that was unknown to them previously. The second type of speaking in tongues is what is commonly practiced in Pentecostal and other charismatic churches today, which is the practice of speaking a heavenly language.

Speaking in tongues, at least in the New Testament sense, is thought of to be utterances of a foreign language that is unknown to the one uttering the message. The idea behind this practice was that the Gospel could be preached supernaturally when the person preaching did not know the native language of those they were speaking to. This means that speaking in tongues should reflect an actual language and not just a melodic utterance of a pseudo-language.

Throughout the rest of history, we see only sporadic testimonies of people speaking in tongues. There are testimonies of missionaries and monks, such as Saint Vincent Ferrer, who participated in or witnessed individuals speaking in tongues. Abbess Hildegard of Bingen claimed to have been able to speak Latin without ever studying the language[12]—even though 12th century theologian Bernard of Clairvaux claimed that tongues were no longer practiced. It was not until the 19th century before communal speaking in tongues became a more common phenomenon. There are various church documents from this time that record when speaking in tongues occurred, particularly in the charismatic denominations like Pentecostalism.

The Indwelling of the Divine Consciousness

Scripture states that those who believe in Jesus Christ as their Lord receive the gift of the Divine Consciousness who indwells the believer while on Earth. "Don't you know that you yourselves are God's temple and that God's Spirit dwells in your midst?"[13]

Scripture also says that our bodies are like a temple where the Divine Consciousness resides: "Do you not know that your bodies are temples of the Holy Spirit, who is in you, whom you have received from God? You are not your own . . ."[14]

Some people understand this passage to mean that each individual has a responsibility to take care of their bodies by living healthy lives, which includes exercise, rest, and eating healthy foods. These things not only make our bodies healthy, but they also make our minds strong. Strong minds and the bodies that contain them are important for the Divine Consciousness to use for the work of the kingdom. This is something we oftentimes fail to keep in mind.

The indwelling of the Divine Consciousness also includes convicting Christians to be active in social justice. The Spirit reminds/enlightens the believer to the reality of what it means to serve those who are oftentimes ostracized by their communities and convicts the individual to intervene to provide assistance and/or activism when necessary.

This Consciousness also connects us on a larger level to the Church. As brothers and sisters, we are all connected through the indwelling of this Consciousness that links its Church together.[15] Whether this is through spiritual gifts or communal prayer, we are linked by this Divine Consciousness as brothers and sisters of faith. However, far too often we treat each other as though we are estranged when we should be united under the Spirit of Truth as ones who genuinely care for one another. The Spirit convicts us to extend that love to those outside of the Church as well.

Christian Existence & Personal Identity

The Divine Consciousness assures us of our future hope; for as long as there is a Divine Consciousness that indwells its Church, then there is the certainty that accompanies the promises that Jesus made to mankind. Jesus is the only one able to provide certainty for his people; for if he is wrong or his promises do not endure, then he is a liar and consequently not Divine. Therefore, we must be assured in the promises that he grants his Church—one such promise is the Divine Consciousness—referred to in Scripture as the Holy Spirit or the "Helper."

Some of these promises are recorded in the Bible, although they may or may not be accurate reflections of what Jesus taught. There is probably a core truth to every statement, parable, and event described in the Bible—with a layer of embellishment on top. (Every time Scripture was rewritten there exists the possibility of embellishment by the scribes who were responsible for copying the Bible.)

The Divine Consciousness describes humans as much as it does the Trinity. In Scripture, we are told that when we decide to follow Jesus, we are given the "Helper" that links them to this greater Christian experience.[16] We are also told that when we decide to follow Jesus that we give up our identity and put on Jesus's identity.[17] The Divine Consciousness helps to facilitate that transition of being. Our "being-in-the-world"[18] must be Spirit-filled in that it alters our self-awareness and identity. To "become" a Christian is a very real, transformative process that we must feel comfortable embracing—and embrace it to the fullest!

The Divine Consciousness does not just manifest itself as an internal witness to the believer. It also projects outwardly in the world as the testimony of the believer. We are told that the Spirit gives power and confidence to the believer to express their faith in Christ to the world. This expression of faith is an act of obedience where word and deed become one.[19]

Prayer

Perhaps the most beautiful yet complicated expression of the Christian faith is prayer. Prayer is the poetic expression of the soul before God and can be used in a variety of ways. However, it has two primary functions; the first is as an act of worship. Prayer can express emotions and aspects of worship that are distinct among more common forms of worship, such as singing. The second, and probably the most common form of prayer, is the petition of requests that God's people have for various events taking place within the life of the Church. God cares deeply for the concerns of his people. Yet, he is not in the business of granting requests like a genie in a bottle. In fact, it seems somewhat arbitrary how and when he seemingly decides to answer prayer requests.

However, Scripture testifies to the value of bringing these questions to God.[20] This is the most significant role that the Divine Consciousness plays in the life of the believer. It acts as the conscious link between humanity and God. It is responsible for indwelling the believer and guiding them into ministry. It gives the individual the power of faith that can move metaphorical mountains.[21] Prayer and faith go hand in hand with one another.

Multiple philosophical issues accompany the act of prayer. Most of these are minor with one exception, "Does prayer change God's mind?" This question has boggled the minds of religious people for centuries. Unfortunately, very little is written on the philosophical issues of prayer.

There are two things to consider when pondering the aforementioned question: first, the question assumes a universe governed by determinism. Determinism refers to a force that determines events that take place in the world. In a world where there is free will, the question is simple to answer: God's Mind need not be changed because he did not ordain said event to occur—free will did.[22] Therefore, one's prayer is not to change God's mind, but rather to ask him to intervene.

The issue becomes complicated if one believes we live in a deterministic world. If you believe that God is directing certain (or all) events to occur in this world, then the question of God changing his mind is very relevant. However, in both cases, the question of the individual's power to reach God is also relevant. Do prayers make it to the mind of God, or do they fall back to Earth like rain? This is a question that has more to do with faith than a philosophical conundrum. Does the individual have faith in the role and power of the Divine Consciousness to speak to God on our behalf?[23]

But what if we do live in a deterministic universe? Certainly, our tiny little human request will not change the mind of God, will it? For God to change a single small event in a deterministic universe would require the reorganization of everything in reality. For example, if God "changed his mind" and chose to heal someone who was dying so that they live longer, then that individual is interacting with the world and changing the events that would have otherwise not occurred without them. Eventually, the effect of that one request is felt around the world. Millions of people pray to God every day. The math is incalculable for the number of contingencies necessary to change the world in a deterministic universe. Therefore, it seems unlikely that prayer changes God's mind in a deterministic universe.

Earlier we talked about the idea that we already live in the best possible world. I touched on prayer in that section, but only briefly. If we do live in the best possible world, then it seems unlikely that prayer has any effect on God. After all, in such a world any change would create a world that was no longer "best", not as good as the one before it. What should we make of prayer if we *are* living in the best possible world? We are told to pray, so what purpose does it actually have in such a world? We'll consider this question and other aspects of prayer in the rest of this chapter.

Despite all the arguments mentioned against it, God does appear to answer prayer at times, even in miraculous supernatural ways. Are those simple coincidences or are we reading into our circumstances? Possibly. This is the paradox of prayer. Unfortunately, there is no good answer to this paradox –

that is why it is a paradox. We are left with two things in this discussion. First, the New Testament is clear that we are to pray without ceasing.[24] Even Jesus prays. We don't have to understand how it works in order to practice it.

Second, prayer has a greater purpose beyond making requests. It is the primary communicative framework between humanity and their Creator. It also affects our being in profound ways. Consider what Kierkegaard said about prayer. "Prayer does not change God; it changes the one who offers it."[25] Kierkegaard meant that prayer is an exercise in spiritual transformation. Like Jesus in the Garden who prays, "not my will but yours be done,"[26] it seems as if the role of prayer is to be transformational as our requests are ultimately subsumed by God's will.

THE IDEA OF PRAYER is a complicated one for progressive Christians. Many are turned off by the practice because so many within Christianity have abused it over the years. For those who do practice it, they often do so as Kierkegaard suggested—as a spiritual exercise in getting centered with the Divine.

Regardless of whether we understand prayer, we cannot deny the biblical evidence that instructs us to do it continuously. Our inability to comprehend its purpose or our aversion to it due to spiritual abuse of the practice, should not prevent us praying. We should still pray in line with our convictions and with the expectation that, at the very least, God will hear our cry.

The Divine Consciousness is involved in every aspect of the Christian life. The indwelling of this Consciousness is vital as it creates the relationship that exists between the Creator of the universe and its creation. Without its presence, we would be wanderers in a dark world. To embrace the role of the Spirit in our lives is to embrace the ways in which God communicates to his people. Life in the Spirit means a life in God who values interaction from his creation.

DISCUSSION QUESTIONS

1. Do you think the Holy Spirit is a legitimate third person of the Trinity? What makes the Holy Spirit unique to other attributes of God?

2. Why do you think it is important for the Holy Spirit to indwell believers?

3. How do you think the Spirit helps to inform our identity?

4. How would you define prayer? Do you think it is necessary?

5. Does prayer change anything?

6

CREATION & HUMANITY

"Every act of creation is first an act of destruction."
— **Pablo Picasso**

"Love is the motive, but justice is the instrument."
— **Reinhold Niebuhr**

THE UNIVERSE IS VAST and deep, full of twinkling stars and swirling galaxies, but this enormous ether has a dark secret: it could have never existed on its own. Its existence is so improbable that there must be some greater force behind its creation. The existence of this creation demands an answer to the question, "Why is there something instead of nothing?" This is what theists have been asking atheists to explain for years. As it turns out, this beautiful creation that we exist in is one of the greatest proofs of God's existence. There is no answer to the question why is there something instead of nothing. But in a theistic worldview, the answer is simple: God!

When we talk about creation in general, we are talking about the *cosmos* (the universe). More specifically, we are talking about the creation account as outlined in the book of Genesis. The creation account in Genesis is perhaps one of the most misunderstood parts of Scripture. Many people have fallen into the trap of reading their own scientific context into the creation account. By attempting to get at the truth behind the truth, many have turned the opening chapters of Genesis into a science textbook.

It is important to understand at the outset that Genesis is not a scientific book. It is not meant to undercut any modern scientific claims. The opening chapters of Genesis are poetic in nature and though they communicate truth, they communicate their own truth. A truth that was truth for the Jews. It was not written for Christians. It was not written for people in our own time. There is no secret code underlying the text. Instead, it is meant to provide a nominal history taking the form of a myth with the explicit purpose of reminding Israel that they serve the one true God. Theologian Gabriel Fackre sums up the creation narrative beautifully.

> Yes, the early writers spoke in the thought-forms of their day and age but did so with a poetic grace meant to lead us past sight to insight. They used the cosmology of their time to express the truth opened to them by the Spirit about who God is and what the world means. The cadences and figures of the Genesis account are theological poetry that leads us to the depths.[1]

The book of Genesis is one book in a group of five known as the Pentateuch (aka the five books or the *Torah*).[2] Genesis is meant to be understood in the context of the whole group of books. Although Moses is credited as being the author of Genesis, the truth is we really don't know. All of the content contained in the Pentateuch was not pulled together and formed until the 6th century BCE. This is relevant because Christians usually read these books as the context for the rest of the Hebrew Scriptures, and yet, probably much of it was produced around the same time as most of the Hebrew Scriptures.

The Torah was also compiled during the Babylonian captivity—a 70-year time period when the Jewish people were taken captive by King Nebuchadnezzar II of Babylon. There are hints of this captivity throughout the narrative. Moreover, the compilation of Genesis—especially, the first 11 chapters—is meant to remind Israel how they wound up in captivity and to provide encouragement that God would be there for them.

This tumultuous context is apparent in Genesis 1 where parallels to the Enuma Elish—the Babylonian creation narrative—are evident. It is for this reason that many scholars believe that Genesis 1 was written during Israel's captivity in Babylon.[3] As an interesting side note, if this is true it would make Genesis 2 older than Genesis 1.

Creation

The theological term for discussing creation is referred to as "General Revelation" or sometimes as "Natural Revelation". It is called this because God reveals himself generally or through natural means in the creation. God gave humanity the creation as a home. Creation not only serves as the abode of humanity, but it also testifies to the power and creativity of its Architect.[4]

Genesis Chapters 1-3 are mythological in nature.[5] With that said, there is a common misconception when it comes to the nature of "myth". Many believe that myths are untrue stories. This is a misunderstanding of the myth genre. Mythology is a narrative category that consists of deeply profound stories that are created about an ancient past.

Many times, myths are built upon multiple truths that are simply extrapolated on through the years, which is often the case with oral histories. One can compare Genesis Chapter 2 with Chapter 1 to see this extrapolation. (Remember, Chapter 2 is older than Chapter 1 so it should be understood in that order.) Moreover, although the chapters are mythological in nature, they also contain historical, philosophical, and theological truths that are important to discern. These stories were not created to be read literally, so readers should allow the text to speak in the way it was intended.

The content of Genesis 1 is straightforward and well organized. It was written with textual breaks distinguished by the phrase "and God said...." Chapter divisions within Scripture are helpful, but they are a Medieval invention. The early Jews and Christians did not have these chapter and verse delineations when they read Scripture. Biblical authors sometimes included natural delineations in order to help the reader better navigate the text. However, in this case, the phrase "and God said . . ." in Genesis 1 is more of a poetic refrain than a natural text break.

The Genesis 1 version of the creation story is very specific and details various elements of creation. Importantly, it distinguishes humans as the final created element—distinct from the rest of the created order. It is clear by reading Genesis 1 that the author is trying to emphasize not only the importance of humanity generally but also how important humanity is to God. This relationship between God and "humanity" is discussed further in the section below.

Genesis 1:1 starts with, "*In the beginning, God* created the heavens and the earth" (emphasis mine). This is of critical importance given the context in which this was written. The Ancient Near East (ANE) was consumed by pluralistic religions. The fact that the Jewish narrative begins with a single powerful deity speaks volumes, especially to the people in the ANE. It indicated to the other religions that YAHWEH can do by himself what it takes their captor's religion multiple deities to achieve. No doubt this communicated to the Jews that their God is omnipotent and that they can trust in his power to free them from their captivity.

Next, is Genesis 2, or perhaps I should say *first* is Genesis 2. When there are comparable narratives that appear in separate documents, it is usually the shortest or more generic narrative that tends to be older. This is the case with

Genesis Chapter 2, which is a more generic version of the creation story than what is presented in Chapter 1.

Just like Genesis 1, the emphasis of Genesis 2 is also on humanity. However, it magnifies God's relationship to humans tenfold from Genesis 1. Some find it problematic that humans are not described as created last in Genesis 2, as it seemingly contradicts Genesis 1. (Many also have issues with the fact that many of the creation elements don't line up between the two chapters either.) However, this is the wrong way to compare the two stories. Genesis 1 and 2 both have humanity as their main focus, but each chapter goes about that emphasis differently. It's important to keep in mind that these are two different documents were probably separated by around a thousand years. Genesis 1 is, in a sense, creating order out of what takes place in Genesis 2.

Our Ecological Responsibility

God made humans caretakers of creation. In the Genesis account, God commissions Adam to tend to the garden. After the Fall, Adam must toil the Earth for his remaining days. Literalists love to claim the creation story happened exactly as written; however, when it comes to being stewards of creation literalists are often quick to make excuses for their contributions to the Earth's destruction. They also often oppose legislation that could help repair the damage to the creation that we all have contributed to.

Earth is a unique beauty within our solar system. It stands out among the other dark and dingy-looking planets as a place full of life and beauty. It's hard to imagine just how fragile this magnificent-looking planet is. Over the millennia, humans have taken advantage of this lovely place, depleted its resources, and lessened its ability to protect itself. Humans have taken the resources that God has given and selfishly squandered them.

It is amazing to think that God created this magnificent universe out of nothing (*ex nihilo*). In one moment, God was all that existed, and then in the next moment "bang" everything else began to form. Every lovely thing we see in the sky by day or by night is the result of the creative hand of God. From the very large, like planets and galaxies, to the very small, like particles and atoms, all are unique creations of a Creator who lavished humanity with everything beautiful. Unlike the attitude of the gods of Babylon, YAHWEH loves his creation. He loves humanity. This is the message the Jews were meant to understand through the creation narratives.

Despite this beauty, Earth continues to be harmed and treated as though its resources are infinite. Earth is less beautiful and less safe than it has ever been. If humans continue to squander resources, then one day the Earth will no longer be able to sustain life. I think it is hard for many evangelicals to see the inevitably of this future if humans do not drastically change the way they live. Many believe that God will intervene or return before it gets that bad. This belief allows them to justify their own destructive role in Earth's demise. It is rare to see any systematic theology address this issue. Most evangelicals fixate on the creation/evolution debate rather than consider the important doctrine of ecological stewardship. Who has time to save Earth from destruction when one must defend literalist interpretations of its origins?

It will take more than occasionally recycling to help heal our planet. Christians should be at the forefront of creating sustainable policies that help to reduce greenhouse gases and improve life on the planet. Only these large-scale changes will help slow, or even reverse, the effects of humanity's destructive tendencies; that is, if we are not already too late.

Ex Nihilo

Theologians often talk about God creating *ex nihilo* (out of nothing) because most Christians throughout history believe that it is important for God to be the Creator of all things. This was probably the intent of the creation account in Genesis 1. People from the other ANE religions had gods who created only out of the foundational matter that already existed. In contrast, the Genesis

1 account states "In the beginning God created the heavens and the earth . . ."6

The poetic depth of Genesis 1 is easily missed by those seeking theological depth from the text that isn't there. For example, why doesn't God create everything at one time? He could have. Instead, God creates a canvas first (the heavens and the earth). From there, he begins to patchwork various aspects of the creation together until his masterpiece is complete. If anything, Genesis 1 shows us that God took his time in creating. How much time God actually took is a contentious matter of debate between evangelicals and, well, everyone else. This will be discussed in more detail later in this chapter. God took the time not because he was worried about creating frivolously, but because he is an Artist and cares deeply for what he creates.

What's more, every element that God created was "good." It was good simply because God created it. In most secular societies, the Earth was not viewed in this way. The Earth simply contained problems that needed to be overcome. Drought hindered crop growth, earthquakes ruined infrastructure, wind damaged structures, etc. There was always some natural problem that people in agrarian societies needed to solve. This was the primary impetus behind the creation of various gods in ancient Mesopotamian culture. For the Jews, it was important for them to know that what God creates is good not simply because God is good, but because God's creation is as well.

Humanity

According to Genesis, humanity was birthed from within the Earth's womb. God fashioned the human being out of the clay of the ground. This poetic description is meant to illustrate the extent to which God was involved in the intricate details of our creation. We are a work of God's art—the pinnacle of his creative expression. Not only are we a product of God's artistic prowess, but our creation also illustrates just how connected to the creation we are. We are a part of the Earth. The Earth not only supports life but at least on one occasion it also created it. And although we have such an intimate connection to the planet we will no doubt one day be responsible for her destruction.

Various Jewish traditions contributed to the book of Genesis. This is why the creation is explained a little differently between Chapters 1 and 2. They are one story from two different traditions. Each story has its own emphasis and purpose. These tales were never intended to be taken literally. They were meant to be taken metaphorically to explain some larger ethic.

For example, the story of Adam and Eve is often taken literally by evangelicals—and more specifically, literalists, to mean that this couple were the first human beings on Earth. Anthropology tells a different story. Adam and Eve are not old enough to be humanity's parents. This leaves two options for understanding Genesis 1 and 2. 1) Maintain the literal stance and jump through anthropological and archeological hoops to make sense of the story, or 2) understand the story metaphorically—as it was intended.

Evolution & Creationism

Evolution and Creationism deserve very little discussion in the context of understanding Genesis because it is misguided to think that this conversation has anything to do with the creation story and is more about competing worldviews. However, given how popular this topic is, I wanted to briefly say a couple of things.

First, the seven days of creation are not necessarily literal 24-hour periods as stated in the story. In fact, archeology proves the Earth is older than five or six thousand years old, which is how old the Earth would be if everything were created in seven days.

Second, Genesis Chapter 2 does not list the created elements in terms of days; it just lists an order. Since Genesis 2 was written first, we can reasonably conclude that the days listed in Chapter 1 are rhetorical devices that go to the heart of the poetic narrative. If the days were important in and of themselves, then Genesis 2 would have also contained them. Regardless, the days are not as important as many modern readers have made them out to be.

Finally, the book of Genesis was not created with science in mind. It was created as a compilation of writings spanning a variety of literary genres. Therefore, anyone trying to make scientific claims or draw scientific conclusions from this text are not interested in the truth of the text itself but are performing their hermeneutics anachronistically. We are uninterested in approaching the biblical text this way.

Adam & Eve Metaphorically

There are two metaphorical options for the story of Adam and Eve: Either they are the first metaphorical Hebrews, or they are the first metaphorical humans. Although a minority position, the idea that Adam and Eve represent the first Hebrews/Jews does have a modest—especially among Jews. After all, the Pentateuch is a Hebrew-centered story. The genealogy of the Hebrews presented in Genesis 5 begins with Adam and Eve as the Hebrew patriarchs and depicts a Hebrew genealogical family. Adam and Eve representing the first Hebrews illustrates a larger ethic; namely, that the Hebrews are set apart because they were intimately created by YAHWEH himself. This theme of being "set apart" is seen throughout the Hebrew Scriptures and culminates in the taking of the promised land.

However, the creation of Adam and Eve *is* presented in the context of the creation of the cosmos. Literal interpretations of Genesis 1 and 2 would support the argument that Adam and Eve were both the first Jews and the first people to be created. However, the scientific evidence that Adam and Eve are not old enough to be humanity's parents outweighs any misguided commitment to literalism in the creation story. This is a hard pill to swallow for literalists as it requires a rethinking of all their beliefs related to the creation of humanity. It also begs the question – if Adam and Eve were representatives of the first Jews—and not the first humans—what does it mean that they were "made in the image of God"? Is this another way that the Jews were set apart? Since it seems absurd that only the Jews would be made in the image of God, then it follows that Adam and Eve must represent humanity and not just the Jews.

Made in God's Image

The creation account described in Genesis 1 says that humans were created "in God's own image". As discussed earlier in this book, we can learn something about the nature of God by reflecting on humanity's nature. Attributes that are unique and necessary for human beings must be, in a Divine way, indicative of the Trinity as well. Two attributes are particularly important to discuss:

First, humans are, at their most basic level, minds in bodies. Upon death, we are at our most basic state—a mind. This same relationship can be seen in the Trinity as well since they are in their oneness, a Divine Mind.

Second, social community is a chief constituent of humans being-in-the-world. Therefore, it must also be the case that the Trinity needs social community among its Divine personhood. It must be necessary as a component in forming the Trinity's identity in some way, as it does with humans.

This departs somewhat from the normal conversation around the image of God. Typically, the debate focuses on the *physical* form humans take versus the *function* humans are meant to have. I argue in Chapter 3 that the *function* of the human being is the chief component of being created in the image of God. We could discuss the human *form*, but I believe this is highly irrelevant to the nature of God's image reflected in humanity. For example, it makes no difference if God has arms or legs or even a head.

An important question for progressive Christians to consider is how human evolution contributes to or takes away from this idea of being made in God's image. Is there a way to reconcile the two ideas? Creative evolution states that evolution is "a creative product of a vital force". I don't think it is far-fetched to think that God was a part of the evolutionary process of creation. In fact, the two seem to be entangled in a perfect dance where they complement each other nicely. The same cannot be said about the physical image of humans. Humans are still evolving. Therefore, if humans are physically made in God's image, then God is never done creating the human. Or put another way, God is never satisfied with how the human is formed. This is a problem.

However, we must also consider that our minds (which are created in the image of God) are also evolving. This should be of greater concern than physical changes since, as I've argued above, it is our invisible qualities that are made in the image of God, qualities such as consciousness, will, and mind.

We must also consider the role Jesus plays in understanding the image of God. Jesus came to Earth at a very specific time in history. Jesus looked like the humans of his time. Early "humans" did not look the same way. Human appearance may also evolve to be something different in the future. Are all manifestations of physical human bodies "made in the image of God"? Was Jesus's human image compatible with all of the forms humanity has taken or will take over its evolutionary life? For all these reasons, it is difficult to reconcile human evolution with humans also being created in the *physical* image of God.

Although this does not comport well with progressive theology's belief in human evolution, we must go where logic and theology take us. As a result, it seems that there must be either some other explanation to make human evolution jive with being created in the physical form of God; or said differently. Human evolution does not seem possible in a worldview shared with a theology that insists we were created in the physical image of God. Therefore, we should be more concerned about the invisible image of God that we were created after and dismiss the single-minded notion of being made in the physical image of the Divine.

To be created in the image of God is to reflect the core characteristics of what it means to be a certain type of being. For the human, we are comprised primarily of minds. As explained in the section on the Trinity, this is the same core constituent for the God-head. Therefore, although human evolution may change our body and our brain, it does not change the core constituent of what it means to be a human – being comprised of a mind/soul.

Equality

Gender is another important factor to consider in any discussion about God's image. The Genesis 2 account is often referenced in conversations about inequality between the genders. The story goes that God creates man first, but man could not handle the work he was commissioned to perform, so God created a *helper* for him. This idea, in particular, is interpreted by some to mean that Eve's primary role in the world was to assist her husband—indicating to some that she is less than him and that her role is to be submissive.

However, "helping" does not necessarily entail a hierarchical relationship. People who claim this assume something that is not present within the text itself; namely, that Adam is in charge when, in fact, God is in charge. Furthermore, Adam recites a beautiful poem that is recorded in Genesis 2:23.

> "This is now bone of my bones
> and flesh of my flesh;
> she shall be called 'woman,'
> for she was taken out of man."

In this passage, Adam asserts the opposite of gender-based hierarchies when he states that she is ". . . bone of my bone . . . flesh of my flesh . . ." He asserts that Eve is coequal to him because she is of him. We will look more into this idea when we talk about personal identity later in the book.

Another part of the equality conversation revolves around whether or not Genesis advocates for heterosexual unions—and, by extension, against anything that is not. This is another example of how many within evangelicalism read the biblical text anachronistically. Genesis 2:24 reads: "That is why a man leaves his father and mother and is united to his wife, and they become one flesh." The only way this is saying that only men and women *must* marry the other sex is if the author is also making the same distinction. The author is not!

First, the author is clearly referring to his previous statement about Eve being of Adam's flesh. The author is performing wordplay as we see in the previous statement that Eve *comes out of* Adam, and in marriage, they are metaphorically put back together.

Second, this is not a prescriptive text. It is describing an event that occurs in marriage.[7] Simply describing an event does not make that event an exclusive representation of the only acceptable form of physical love. This is called presumptiveness or the fallacy of presumption, and it happens all too often in evangelical theology. This occurs when the reader assumes certain things about a text that is not present within the text itself or weren't a part of the author's intent. We should be very cautious with our presumptions about the text. Presumptuousness is not dangerous in and of itself and can, at times, be insightful. However, it can become dangerous when we give more weight to presumptuous thinking than we do to other ideas that have a stronger evidentiary base.

Personal Identity

The creation story can inform how we understand our own personal identity, as well as that of the Trinity. The story of Adam and Eve reveals something very important about personal identity. In Genesis 2, Adam fruitlessly searches everywhere for a helper—one who is like him. God needs to make someone who is like him. Enter Eve. Adam sees himself reflected back in

Eve, ". . . bone of my bone . . . flesh of my flesh . . ." Adam's identity is not made whole until he looks in the eyes of another who is like him. This reflection is not exclusive to marriage. In fact, the reflection that occurs to complete personal identity is the reflection of *humanity* that Adam finds in Eve. This can occur in marriage, but it also occurs in the reflected humanity that Eve presents to Adam. It is why the "other" is so important! Because we empathetically see ourselves in another.

This idea that identity is fully formed through the "other" is similar to Paul Ricoeur's philosophy, "*Oneself as Another*"[8], and his idea of narrative identity found in his book, *Time and Narrative*.[9] Ricoeur postulates that humans find their selfhood in the "sameness" that is contained within another person. This stands in contradiction to what Descartes postulated, which was that selfhood is found internally, *cogito ergo sum,* (I think, therefore I am).

The idea that we find significance in the "other" is a beautiful reminder of how important other people are. They are important not just because they are important to God, but because they are intrinsically important. Our neighbor needs us, and we need our neighbor. This play between neighbor and self also reminds us that we are all equal because we all need each other equally. Society often tells us differently, but in the overall narrative of our lives, all kinds of people are responsible for helping to develop our identity. When we ask the question, "Who am I?" we are, in part, saying I am part of my family; I am part of my neighbor; I am part of my spouse; I am part of my children. When we are talking about personal identity changing throughout our lives, we are talking in part about our *persistence.* That is, how do I change throughout my life? Every day, there is the possibility of a new me because every day we encounter people who leave a little bit of themselves with us. There is an argument to be made here that the more different types of people that we encounter the more our personal identity will be transformed into something greater than it was before.

Christians ought to have an appreciation for who they are in light of who God is (concerning his image) and in light of who their neighbor is (selfhood). This is the most complete picture of what it means to be human. It is why Jesus expressed both during his ministry. In Matthew 22:37–39 he reminds us:

> Jesus replied: "Love the Lord your God with all your heart and with all your soul and with all your mind." This is the first and greatest commandment. And the second is like it: "Love your neighbor as yourself."

For the Hebrew, this meant that YAHWEH's people should always be looking toward God to remind them of *who they are* and looking to their fellow Jews as a reminder of *what they are*. There has been no greater incident to distort human identity than the event of the "Fall". The Fall also separated us from our Creator in ways we cannot possibly conceive.

The Fall

The Fall is one of the major foundational doctrines of the Christian faith. The famous story involves Adam, Eve, and a snake whereby a forbidden piece of fruit is consumed in the Garden of Eden, and humanity is cursed forever. Traditionally, this story recorded in Genesis 3 has been used to justify ideas like total depravity and atonement theories like penal substitution. Most people come to these conclusions if they read the Fall in light of sin, instead of in light of disobedience and separation from God.

It is important to understand that the story of the Fall is mythological, just as the first two chapters of Genesis are. Again, this does *not* mean that elements of the story are *all* false, but rather that it was primarily written to communicate a larger ethic. It takes some hermeneutic pressure off to understand the story as a myth. One no longer must account for every detail of the story. Instead, the author emphasizes broader themes within the story.

The two prevailing narratives about the Fall offer very different perspectives. I will refer to the first as the "sin narrative". This is the traditional evangelical narrative. It begins with humanity existing in complete harmony with the creation and the Creator. Adam and Eve are told they could eat of any tree except the one placed in the middle of the Garden - the Tree of the Knowledge of Good and Evil. After much deliberation (metaphorically, a snake), they chose to fulfill their own desires to eat the fruit over obeying God's will. As a result, they were kicked out of the Garden and estranged from God. In the sin narrative version, this estrangement was necessary because God is unable to coexist with sin. From here, the rest of the Hebrew Scriptures document humanity's sinful nature and how humanity's need for God is born out of the recognition of that nature.

In the sin narrative, we are confronted with a profound question: If sin was the detrimental component that excluded humanity from fellowship with God in the Garden, then why do Adam and Eve remain in the Garden for a time after eating the fruit? If it is true that God cannot be in the presence of sin, and that this is the main reason Adam and Eve were expelled from the Garden, then why are they not kicked out right away? Instead, they have time to hide. When God does arrive, he doesn't immediately send them away from his presence. Instead, he takes great care of them by killing an animal and making garments for them to cover their nakedness. God is in the presence of their "sin" during this time! Moreover, it is not entirely clear why sin is considered the predominant theme in this story.

The second narrative I will refer to is the "reconciliation narrative." In this version of the story, humanity exists in a mutual partnership with God. Humanity's relationship is complete and symbiotic. Everything in the aforementioned story still takes place; the only difference is the elements that are emphasized. Reconciliationists don't deny that sin exists or that it was even present during the story. Instead, they see humanity as introducing *concupiscence*[10] into the world. That is, instead of humanity having a totally depraved sin nature, they are merely *prone* to sin after the Fall, and as a result, all humans sin.

Reconciliationists see three major estrangements taking place as a result of Adam and Eve's decision to "eat the fruit" (disobey God). The first estrangement is between *God and Man*.[11] The second estrangement is between *Adam and Eve* through the discovery of their nakedness and the subsequent shame they feel.[12] Finally, estrangement between *humanity and nature* is illustrated through the consequences humanity *and* nature receive as a result of eating from the tree.[13] Reconciliationists believe these alienations are what need to be overcome at the cross.[14]

The chief ethic demonstrated in the Fall is the same regardless of which narrative one espouses. Humans violated God's will and that act resulted in separation from him. There is a clear parallel between this understanding of the Fall and the purpose of the Incarnation. Jesus proclaims that he came not to save people from sin, but rather to do the will of God.[15] He is also referred to as the second Adam.[16] His life demonstrated what "life-together"[17] looks like for those who follow God. Jesus promises restoration and reconciliation between humanity and God, humanity and humanity, and humanity and nature.

I argued in Chapter 3 that the greatest attribute of the Trinity is their communal relationship. Humans, as image-bearers, also thrive in community—both with God and with each other. It is easy to see why the breaking of community between God and humans is of the utmost consequence. Adam and Eve's exile from the Garden is a metaphor for humanity wandering away from God. This is illustrated soon after in Genesis 4 when Adam & Eve's son, Cain, murders his brother, Abel. Humanity was unable to find their way back to the Garden where they once had fellowship with God. And in their lostness, sin abounds. In their wandering, God's Will is ignored.

The Fall raises several tangential questions that must be addressed for us to understand the nature of the Fall better. To what extent are humans fallen? Is "fallen" even an appropriate term to describe what has happened? Perhaps humans are in a continual state of "falling". To what extent did the Fall deteriorate humanity's relationship with God and to what extent did the reconciliation of Christ bring us back to God? Most importantly, how has the Fall affected humans as image-bearers of God?

Humans are made in the image of God as minds in bodies. As a mind, we reflect the Trinity's nature as a Divine Mind. However, the Fall brought noetic consequences affecting humans' proximity to God. The farther humanity wanders from God, the greater the noetic rift—the greater the sin. Both this noetic rift and sin make it impossible for humans to return to God on our own. We are too lost.[18]

Humanity's inability to come back to God through the course of biblical history demonstrated just how necessary it was for God to come to us. In the Old Testament, God attempted nearness through the judges, the kings, and the prophets, but all to no avail. Therefore, for us to be reconciled to God, God must first come to us because we are hopelessly lost. We are unable to find him on our own.

People are nearest to God when they are in community and doing life-together. The reconciliation of Christ not only demonstrated how one is to live within the will of God, but it also mended the rift between humanity and God through the Holy Spirit. Moreover, doing life-together is what keeps us closest to God. When we refuse to be in community, we are rejecting what God has put in place to keep us accountable to one another. We were never meant to wander. We were meant to be together.

Our identity was not the only thing affected by the Fall. Our ability to make right decisions was severely also altered. This is the notion of free will. The theological question is, "To what extent has my freedom been affected by the Fall."

Free Will

Free will is a philosophical category that has to do with the ability of humans to make choices between at least two distinct options. God planted a forbidden Tree in the middle of the Garden to illustrate that people had free will to choose whether they would be obedient or not. In other words, free will existed *before* the Fall. Humanity cannot exercise free will unless God gives them a choice. This demonstrates that the fruit is just a placeholder for some larger test—*choice*. Would we trust God or seek out answers for ourselves?

The dilemma of the Tree also demonstrates that people will always choose the Tree in the middle of the Garden over God if given the choice. This proved true over and over throughout the Hebrew Scriptures, as well as in the New Testament. People will always doubt whether God has their best in mind. They will always trust themselves over God. Moreover, faith is the choice one makes to follow God over and above choosing themselves. All steps of faith are choices we make. They are meant to bring us closer to God.

Determinism is a key issue related to free will. Determinism refers to the extent to which God determines human actions in the world. Some people believe that God dictates everything in human history. This is referred to as "hard determinism." Some people believe that God is in control of major events and that we have some freedom within those confines. This is referred to as "soft determinism." Some further believe that we have complete free will over all events. In theological circles, determinism is a part of "Calvinism"—named after the French theologian John Calvin (1509-1564).

There are many consequences for those holding to a deterministic worldview. For example, it requires the belief that the Fall was pre-arranged by God. However, this drastically undermines human responsibility for the rift that exists between humanity and God. Determinists argue that if God has foreknowledge, then it must follow that the events he knows about he also brought about. After all, they argue, God cannot foreknow something without having also determined it. The logic is that if God sees an event in the future, then it must become an event in the real world. And, if it becomes an event in the real world and God determines everything then he must have determined the future event he foresaw.

However, free will was necessary for humanity to have because it was necessary for Christ to have. Christ needed to be free in order for his acts of righteousness to be accomplished out of that freedom. Forcing Christ to act a certain way pays no penalty for sins; it provides no scapegoat for wrath; it makes no reconciliation between God and man. Equally important is that free will makes sense of evil in the world, which we discussed earlier in the section on the problem of evil.

If Christ required free will for his mission on Earth to be accomplished and if he reflected the nature of humanity, then we must also have that same freedom. We are not compelled to follow God. Instead, God presents himself to us and we choose whether or not to follow him.

THERE IS A SIGNIFICANT difference between the way evangelicals and progressives view the creation narratives. Much of it has to do with how the Fall is understood and whether it emphasizes a need for redemption or reconciliation. Moreover, since creation is the foundation for the biblical narrative, it colors how people understand the narrative moving forward. This is especially true when we arrive at the Incarnation, consider the ministry of Jesus, and seek to understand his death and subsequent resurrection.

There is much that can be learned from the creation narratives, but they are not meant to be understood scientifically. Instead, their emphasis is on humanity and the situation that humanity finds itself in. When we read ideas into the text that are not present within the intent of the author, we do a disservice to the impact of Scripture.

If you grew up in an evangelical church, then it is likely much of what you understand about the Bible has to do with sin—especially within the Hebrew Scriptures. The Hebrew Scriptures are not as much about sin and sacrifice as they are about how God seems both far (transcendent) and near (imminent) at various times in their history. This doesn't just apply to the Hebrews but to us as well. Often our faith is in constant flux with feelings that God is sometimes near and sometimes far. If we are to praise God for one thing, it should be that he has reconciled humanity unto himself and that this will be fully realized when we become present in the new Garden—the Kingdom of God.

DISCUSSION QUESTIONS

1. Do you think there is a theological mandate to take care of our planet? If so, why does God want us to be good stewards of our planet?

2. What do you think it means to be made in the image of God?

3. Do you think the creation of humanity demonstrates a subordination between men and women or equality? How would you argue against the other perspective?

4. Do you believe in determinism, free will, or a hybrid version of the two?

7

CHURCH, CULTURE & THE CHRISTIAN LIFE

"Your life as a Christian should make non-believers question their disbelief in God.
— ***Dietrich Bonhoeffer***

"Church is too often the most risky place to be spiritually honest."
— ***Peter Enns***

HUMANS ARE LIVING ORGANISMS. They are precarious at times and have certain needs to ensure that they thrive. Humans need relationships. They need to feel connected to other people who care for them. They need to feel important to friends and family. But, perhaps even greater than all of this, humans need to feel loved.

Humans need other humans to function at their highest level. In fact, the core notion of identity can be seen as the reflection of one individual towards another.[1] The idea that personal identity is developed as we see ourselves in other people is one of the most beautiful and practical theories that exists. As we explored in the previous chapter, it's not just beautiful, but it's true.

When a group of people are united—both in their personal identity as humans and as Christ-followers, great things can happen. This was the purpose of the Church when it first formed. The idea was that a group of people would come together with the common bond of knowing Jesus and the desire to make him known. They would share resources, and, in some cases, they even lived communally. Their goal was to share the Gospel among their fellow Jews (at first, then the Gentiles). For these early Christians conversion was as simple as getting baptized and attending communal gatherings. This was the start of what would soon become the institutional Church.

Church

What is the Church? This is the central question of Ecclesiology. There are two primary ways the Church expresses itself in evangelicalism. First, the Church is primarily confessional. That is, its orthodoxy is built around historical creeds and confessions. Second, the Church consists of a community of people who participate in the common worship of God including sacramental communion.[2]

Perhaps the biggest issue that arises from the traditional view of the Church is that it imagines the Church as a group of people gathered together in a central location that then goes out to perform the act of missions in the world. Although this is the historical practice of the Church, it is not the way that Jesus practiced discipleship. Herein lies the difference between evangelical and progressive thinking. That is, evangelicals largely believe that the Church should reflect the Early Church in the New Testament. Although there is no consensus among progressives, they are more apt to look to the life of Jesus and then from there imagine what the Church should look like.

I believe we should reimagine the Church in terms of discipleship. That is, the Church should be training people in the ways of Jesus so that people can imitate Jesus to the world. Discipleship should be most concerned about praxis and not education as its primary function. Education involves the transfer of information from one to another. Knowledge transformed into wisdom was the practice of Jesus in the world. The first church was not organized in Acts. It was organized when Jesus chose his disciples. That group formed the first Christian church and they were largely focused on praxis.

The Early Church was merely an experiment for new Christians who were trying to figure out what it looked like to be a believer under Roman occupation. This the key problem with looking to the New Testament church as a template for how the Church should exist today. Unfortunately, persecution of these early believers forced them indoors and, in some cases, underground (well, not literally). Since persecution was largely ongoing until the time Constantine (who famously converted to Christianity after seeing a cross displayed in the clouds), it made sense that when the Church emerged from the dust it would already be institutionalized. In fact, its institutionalization can be seen as far back as the Jerusalem Council. However, this institutionalization looked much different back then than it does today.

Regardless, the Church is made up of individuals who carry the Church with them wherever they go. Their time of gathering as a community for worship was secondary to the primary purpose of a lived ecclesiastical existence *within* the world. This is not to say that the gathering of believers is not important. As previously mentioned, the gathering acts as the epicenter for discipleship. That is the learning, mentoring, and missional activity of the individual. All of these aspects come together into a single experiential entity called the Church.

This is in stark contrast to the programmatic nature of the evangelical church which stresses the cognitive aspects of learning over and above those that are more experiential. The Church must be more than entertainment. It must be more than something performed exclusively on Sunday mornings. It must be more than a dogmatic institution. Instead of requiring others to be a certain way before entering the doors, the Church must be dynamic and willing to *transform itself* into whatever the culture *needs*. It is not a compromise to meet the needs of the people that you are ministering to; it is the way of Jesus.

The Church, as Jesus intended, is a reimagining of Israel. It is Israel as it was intended to be. Despite all of its flaws, the Church is still needed. It still has a purpose in the world. Jesus says that the Church will always exist and ". . . not even the gates of hades will overcome it."[3] For better or worse, we need to accept the fact that the Church is what early believers formed. Although it is what we have, it doesn't need to be stale and ineffective. We have to remember that although the Church is an institution, it is also made up of people. And when like-minded people get together, they can do incredible things.

How Christians Believe

There is a progression from how most Christians *come to believe* in God to what maintains their *ongoing belief*. For many, the things that originally convinced them to become Christian are not enough to sustain their faith. They need more. The simple ideas of the faith are eventually added to by the deeper things of God as they transition from one phase to the next, to the next, etc. Some Christians leave behind the elementary ideas that originally convinced them to believe for a weightier theology. Those early beliefs are the foundation for how they continue to develop their theology. Moreover, regardless of their veracity, many continue to build new theology upon those foundational beliefs. But what if that foundation is fraught with deeply flawed ideas and assumptions? What if those beliefs come into conflict with newer revelations? Suddenly, doubt threatens what was once so absolute in our minds. This likely sounds familiar, either because you've known people who've taken this unsettling journey or you've been on or are contemplating it for yourself. Enter a book on deconstructing and reconstructing one's faith to guide these travelers through (winky face).

It's important to remember that in most cases we do not come to our core beliefs on our own. We are never taught *how* to believe, instead we are often told *what* to believe. This method of indoctrinating new believers is dangerous as it has denied many the tools necessary for self-discovery—and impacted more than just new converts. Indoctrination is a problem for mature believers as well. Many in the Church have become lazy believers, needing to have their spiritual food fed to them, instead of growing up and feeding themselves. This is none the more evident in today's largely uninformed Western Christian culture.

This lack of spiritual independence has created a dependency on pastors and teachers. It leads to psychological phenomena like "group-think," which we see paraded throughout our culture – especially during and after the Trump presidency. From participating in an insurrection to refusing vaccines, evangelical lay people have become puppets to evangelical leaders largely due to their inability to think critically. Critical thinking gives an individual the tools needed to evaluate the information they are taking in, but evangelical pastors typically do not create environments for this to happen.

Heaven & Hell

People with experience in evangelicalism, like me, will usually remember the day they "accepted Jesus as their personal savior" in order to get into Heaven. After all, they were taught that all people are destined for Hell simply by being born - unless they repent of their sins and accept Jesus. In other words, it makes no difference within this worldview what humans do while on Earth, only whether they have accepted Jesus as their "savior" or not. Who wouldn't want to get in line to sign up for Heaven when presented this way? Of course, evangelicals do not evangelize this way, but it is where the logic leads.

However, what is missing from this conversation is the difficulty of being a Christian, especially if one does it correctly. It's not all angels and harps. It costs something to be a disciple of Jesus Christ—and, no, I'm not talking about cries of faux-Christian persecution in the West. I'm talking about the very real struggle of living an authentically Christian life. This struggle needs to be a bigger part of the conversation.

The "Get-Out-of-Hell-Free Card" narrative is deeply rooted within evangelicalism to this day. It is the emphasis on the afterlife that perpetuates a faith that is "Heaven-centric." It enforces the idea that all work done on Earth will eventually award the believer with "treasures in Heaven."[4] This incentive can often take the heart out of the work Christians are to do and lead people who perform acts of service for selfish reasons—or as we used to say, for "fire insurance."

It is easy within a worldview like this to direct the attention away from the things of Earth to the things of Heaven. Unfortunately, this can lead some Christians to neglect stewardship of creation and social justice, as such acts are deemed inconsequential to eternity. The problem with this mindset is that Heaven is a place on Earth, not a place in some ethereal spirit realm. Is that not what we are referring to when we talk about the Kingdom of God?[5] At the very least, this should give some pause when considering involvement in stewardship of the Earth and humanitarian work.

Another question we must consider is whether Hell is even a real place? If it is, then who gets sent there and for how long? Many progressives and most evangelicals will agree that there has to be a place where wrongs are made right and that there should be some sort of justice for whatever evils were perpetrated against humanity and God while on Earth. Where progressives and evangelicals often disagree is on the duration of this punishment (or refinement, as some prefer to say).

Eternal Hell is a prominent doctrine within the evangelical narrative. This idea comes primarily from a couple of verses like Matthew 25:46, which states ". . . then they will go away to eternal punishment, but the righteous to eternal life."[6] However, none of the many other passages that refer to Hell (or Hades), refer to it as being eternal.

The Greek for "eternal punishment" is *aionios kolasis*. In his book, *Atheist Delusions: The Christian Revolution and Its Fashionable Enemies*,[7] theologian and philosopher David Bentley Hart argues that the early Greek Fathers would not have interpreted *aionios* as "eternal." Instead, they would have understood it as "a long period of time," which Hart suggests is the correct understanding of the term.

However, if this is true, then how should Christians understand the second part of the aforementioned verse where "eternal" is used to describe those who will have eternal life? Does it mean that eternal life is not really eternal, but just a prolonged period of time? It doesn't make much sense to suggest that Heaven is just a prolonged period of time. Although usage is important for understanding Greek, context is just as important, and the context here doesn't seem to warrant Hart's understanding of the text.

The question that evangelicals have to consider is whether or not God is a being of justice. If he is, then no one warrants eternity in Hell—not even the likes of Adolph Hitler. Another theoretical option that exists is an idea called annihilationism. In this view, once the individual has served their time in some non-Heaven-like place, then justice is complete and the soul is annihilated and no longer exists.

The view that many progressives hold is called universalism. This is the idea that since God desires that all people be saved,[8] while at the same time being just, Hell must be a time of refinement and not necessarily punishment. And that those who complete this process will eventually be in Heaven.

Universalism

We are all humans. We are all on a journey in our lives. Some of us care more about religion and the role it plays in life than others. Not all religions are created equal. Some get us closer to the truth than others do. Ultimately, we all die, and curiosity about the afterlife is a very human question to consider. Some do not believe in an afterlife at all, but for many, it's an important aspect of what gives them hope. Inevitably, humans seek an understanding of the afterlife and the role that religion may or may not play in getting one to the right kind of afterlife.

Universalism—the belief that eventually, all people will end up in Heaven—has been debated since the Middle Ages. Before that time, almost everyone was a universalist in some way, whether as an annihilationist or some other view. The same debate about the afterlife has heated up (pun intended) within progressive Christianity as well. The debate centers around the question of whether or not Hell is real? If it is, to what extent do people get sent there and why?

Most progressives are, to some extent, universalists, but what exactly does it mean to be a universalist? There are many different views under this umbrella of universalism. The version that I'm interested in here is referred to as "universal reconciliation". This refers to the belief that in some way everyone will eventually be reconciled to God and will find themselves in Heaven.

There is a very simple argument for why this is likely to be true. The idea of spending eternity in Hell is unjustifiable by any logical measurement. There is nothing an individual can do throughout their limited life to warrant spending eternity in Hell. Is this just speculation or is this belief supported by Scripture? Part of the argument is related to logic. Out of all the passages that describe Hell in one way or another, there are only a couple of verses that describe Hell as eternal.[9] "Then they will go away to eternal punishment, but the righteous to eternal life" (Matthew 25:46).

However, Matthew also records this, "Do not be afraid of those who kill the body but cannot kill the soul. Rather, be afraid of the One who can destroy both soul and body in Hell" (Matthew 10:28). This verse could be read to support the idea of "annihilationism." I mention this passage because it is not entirely clear what position is being advocated for since two contradictory perspectives are mentioned. This presents a logical problem for eternal punishment. In general, when this happens either the author is being logically inconsistent, or he means something different than what we think he means. However, what we do know is that both interpretations of the afterlife cannot be true.

There are two ways that Hell can exist and still maintain some form of logical coherence: Annihilationism, which we've already discussed, or apocatastasis, one type of universalism. Both support the idea of Hell as a form of restoration. This idea leans heavily into the analogy of fire as a source of refinement instead of punishment. However, where annihilationism claims destruction after this refinement, apocatastasis supports the idea of "universal restoration." Once a person has done their time, they have been refined into something that can exist within Heaven. Although this perspective has some historical precedence, it is also highly speculative since there is no real biblical basis for it. Church Fathers from both the East and the West have held this view, for example, Origen, Clement of Alexandria, Gregory of Nyssa, Jerome, Peter Chrysologus, Maximus the Confessor, and Gregory of Nazianzus.

That leaves us with the question of whether there is any positive evidence for universal reconciliation, a form of universalism that argues that everyone will be reconciled to God, but unlike apocatastasis, this form of universalism denies the existence of Hell. Many will use 2 Peter 3:9 to defend this belief,[10] "The Lord is not slow in keeping his promise, as some understand slowness. Instead, he is patient with you, not wanting anyone to perish, but everyone to come to repentance."

If it is true that God wishes for all to come to knowledge of him, then there should be some mechanism in place for him to accomplish this. God is omnipotent, so it seems that whatever he desires should come to pass. Other passages that act as positive evidence for universal reconciliation include John 12:32, Acts 13:19-21, 1 Corinthians 15:28, 2 Corinthians 5:18-19, Colossians 1:19-20, 1 Timothy 2:3–4, and 1 Timothy 4:10.

Universal reconciliation is Jesus-centric. In John 10 Jesus gives the parable of the good shepherd. This parable describes a shepherd who led his sheep to life by the mere sound of his voice. He calls them and they listen and follow him. Jesus is the Good Shepherd, not wanting anyone to perish. He calls us and leads us *all* to life.

The Role of Women in Church & Society

The amount of time dedicated to debating the roles of women in Church and society is incalculable. Everything that can be said about the issue has been said and said again. This begs the question, why are we still talking about this? Why do many denominations still limit the role of women in ministry?

Historical context is important to consider when reading Scripture, especially for this issue. For most of human history, the role of women in society was largely based on their role within the family. In fact, it wasn't until the "Age of Reason" (16th century) that this began to slowly change as the chief capital of Western society shifted to be more intellectually-based, rather than physically-based. Women were still treated as unequal to men, but they had more public opportunities for engaging in intellectual discussion.

Early human cultures were largely agrarian—or agricultural—in nature. Since men are generally bigger and physically stronger, they focused primarily on manual labor while women often focused on childbearing and rearing, as well as other household tasks. This created a "natural" separation of roles between the genders in a time when it was necessary to survive.

It should be noted that not all societies operated this way. Some societies existed that were not gender-based, and women were free to pursue various roles in those societies. There are several examples that one could point to, such as the Nubia (Kush) region of Africa. Although not always run by women, Queens ruled for much of its history and women exercised important roles within government.[11] This is illustrated through the childhood of Augustine who was raised by a Nubian mother who converted her rebellious son to Christianity. Although more dispersed geographically than they once were, a matrilineal society continues today among the Nubian people.[12] The Palawan society, an indigenous ethnic group located in the Philippines, has no gender hierarchy and never has. The Khasi people of India have always had a matriarchal society with three notable traditions: After marriage, husbands go to live with their wife's community, children typically take on the name of their mother, and daughters receive the inheritance, not sons.[13] Although these types of societies are not common, they have existed, and some still exist today.

The Greek philosopher Aristotle provides us a glimpse into how women were viewed in ancient times in several of his writings. In his work *Politics*,[14] Aristotle says, "The relation of male to female is by nature a relation of superior to inferior and ruler to ruled." He speaks about this more in his work, *History of Animals*:[15]

> Women are too often managed by their emotions, prone to depression, and fight too much among themselves . . . Unlike men who are eager to help those in need and are brave in the face of danger.

Things did not get much better for women in Roman society as they were often viewed as property. (This relates primarily to the commoner as there were high-ranking, upper-class women who were not treated this way.) However, when the Church made its way onto the scene, things changed. Suddenly, men were charged with loving their wives, and women were viewed as having value because they were worthy of that affection.

Societal gender norms based solely on biological differences were called into question on a larger scale after the Industrial Revolution when many economies transitioned from agrarian to industrial in nature. Intellectual capital gained in importance and suddenly women could consider a different path in life other than (or in addition to) childbearing and rearing. Advancements in medical technology also made pregnancy and childbirth safer for women and post-natal recovery times shorter on average.

Many men scrambled to uphold the status quo in order to maintain their power and control. After all, societal gender norms are more about the fragile egos of men than anything else—or so it seems. Some men resorted to insulting the intellectual integrity of women who were often denied formal education in their youth in favor of boys. From attributing witchcraft to progressive women in early American history to selling elixirs to treat "hysteria" during the Civil War, women have often been met with resistance when they dared to question strict social structures, even in a country that boasted that all people are created equal. If it weren't for the pioneering efforts of the suffrage movement in the early 20th century and feminist leaders in the 1960s—whose relentlessness challenged the patriarchal power brokers—who knows where women's rights would be at in this country.

So, what about those pesky Bible passages that seem to diminish the role of women in the home and the Church? Sociological and cultural context is important when evaluating biblical passages that address the roles of women. There are two primary areas where complementarians argue for the role-based subordination of women. The first is the Genesis argument, which boils down to the order of human creation. The second is the apostolic argument, citing many of the New Testament passages that suggest gender-based roles. These perspectives are often argued together to prove that the issue of women in the Church and society has continuity between the Hebrew Scriptures and the New Testament.

Complementarians often argue that Genesis demonstrates that men and women were created with specific purposes and roles. They will mention everything from the fact that woman was created second to Eve's role in the Fall, as proof that women were made to take a subordinate role in church and society. As discussed in the section on creation, this is not a proper understanding of the creation narratives.

Rather than argue the details of each passage (which I think has merit in the right context), there are two simple arguments against this complementarian logic. First, those that make the Genesis argument do so under the assumption that this part of Genesis is *prescriptive* (giving a command) when in fact the entire book was meant to be read descriptively (describing historical events, sometimes utilizing metaphor to do so). In other words, the purpose of Genesis was to record the oral history of the Jews, not to give commands.

The second argument against complementarian logic asks the question, "Why do complementarians point to humanity *post-Fall* as the example that God set forth for men and women? Doesn't it make more sense to look at their *pre-fall* state to understand what God's intention was for humanity? If anything is clear it is that men and women were created in God's image; there is no subordination, no inequality in God. Therefore, there is no subordination or inequality between men and women. (Note: The idea of Trinitarian subordination is an unbiblical, speculative theory that was created to enhance the idea that Genesis teaches the subordination of women. This topic is covered in the section on the Trinity.)

There are also New Testament passages that complementarians use to prove their case for gender-based hierarchy. Most of the passages state in some way that a woman cannot have authority over a man (for example, 1 Cor 14:34-35 and 1 Tim 2:12). These passages do seem "prescriptive," so what should we make of them? Believe it or not, many of these passages *do* affirm that woman cannot have authority over a man. However, what they *say* and what they *mean* for us today are two different things. Context should always dictate what the passage is communicating to the readers of that time. And in this case, context is everything! The context dictates whether or not a particular passage is cultural (only applies to the culture in which the passage was written) or universal (applies to everyone regardless of their position in history).

The passages noted above refer to the immediate context in which they were written and are not meant to be universal axioms. The reason they are included in the New Testament is not entirely clear from the passages alone.

However, there are several reasons to believe these passages reflect a cultural construct.

First, it is believed by many scholars that this particular verse is an interpolation of a later scribe. There is good reason to think this is true. The most convincing fact is that what has been traditionally understood as being 1 Corinthians 14:34-35 sometimes appears at the end of chapter 14 instead of the middle. This inconsistency is a trademark of a notation from a scribe that has made its way into the text.[16]

Second, there is no inherent deficit in women that warrants this subordination. Women are just as intellectually capable as men. It makes more sense to consider that Paul gave these instructions to churches for a specific reason - perhaps to avoid raising the suspicion of Roman leaders who would find the idea that women are equal repulsive.

Third, in some of Paul's other epistles, he refers to "everyone" or "all" can teach/preach/instruct/lead worship, etc. For example, 1 Cor 14:31—which ironically, is the same passage that also states that women are to remain silent, indicating that he means something different when he addresses women specifically.

Fourth, there are women leaders in the Early Church as noted in the New Testament. What's more, Paul, the same author who wrote 1 Corinthians and 1 Timothy clearly holds some of these women in high esteem as indicated in Romans.[17]

Fifth, Jesus had female apostles, which gave them enormous authority over non-apostles. For example, Mariamne, Irene, Nino, Thecla, Phoebe, Prisca, and Junia.[18]

Therefore, unless Paul's writings are contradictory to the rest of Scripture, then there must be important contextual information we are not given. It seems to me that there is more to the story that we are unaware of. The passages that seem to promote women having a distinct, subordinate role from men were based upon the agrarian culture of the time, which no longer persists in much of the world. Ultimately, this means that these passages are not universal, but have application only to those in the ANE.

The Church can neither understand the Gospel, nor its implications for the world, until it *fully* embraces the gifts of *all* members of God's kingdom. For most of Christian history, the Church suppressed half of its intellectual capacity by denying women any place in church leadership. We need women's voices, not only to help us better understand the Gospel, but also to help propel the ministry of the Church into the current cultural milieu. Without women, we will never fulfill our potential as the Church. Without women, our preaching of the Gospel is in vain.

Being Pro-Life Instead of Anti-Abortion

Those within the "pro-life" movement are not really "pro-life" as much as they are "anti-abortion." On the surface, it may not appear that there is not much of a difference. However, the differences that exist are important distinctions to understand.

I think most people would agree that life is precious and precarious. So fragile is this life that humans are given 70 years (if we are lucky) to leave our fingerprints on the records of history. Without life, the universe and everything contained therein are devoid of meaning. Therefore, life and its persistence are not just important, but also necessary. Furthermore, *all* human life is of special importance, not just specific ones.

Ever since Roe v. Wade, the most significant political issue for many Christians has been the issue of abortion. For many of the so-called "pro-lifers", the issue is simple, maybe even axiomatic. And because the issue of abortion is a legislative one, religious folks (of whom most of the "pro-life" movement consists of) must align themselves with those politicians who will support a "pro-life" agenda. For many of these individuals (usually conservative Catholics and Evangelicals), there is no greater sin than to cast your vote for anyone other than a "pro-life" candidate. As the presidential election of 2016 showed us, it makes no difference how sinful the candidate or their policies are, as long as they are deemed "pro-life."

The "pro-life" movement was designed as a smokescreen by evangelical theologian Francis Schaeffer and his son, Frank, as a way to develop political allies under a common banner. It had no real foundation in theology. That part was later developed as a way to better solidify the belief for the Church. However, in reality, there is no real Scripture that supports this political belief. That doesn't mean someone shouldn't be "pro-life," as long as they understand what they mean when they say that.

Up to this point, the word "pro-life" has been carefully qualified with quotation marks. This is because I would like to suggest that many within this movement are not "pro-life"; they are "anti-abortion." The reason that "pro-life" is a misnomer for many is that the life that they advocate for is very specific—the unborn. Many of these individuals and groups believe that even the mother's health is secondary to that of the unborn.

To be pro-life in a non-parenthetical way means that you support all measures that aid in the persistence of innocent life. The irony of many in the anti-abortion movement is that the unborn takes primacy above and beyond all other types of life. Below are a few examples.

Adoption – The number one alternative that anti-abortion supporters advocate for is adoption. Yet, there are an estimated 122,000 children in the U.S. foster care system who are eligible for adoption[19] and only about 5% of practicing Christians in the United States have adopted.[20]

Immigration – According to Pew there were 10.5 million Asylum seekers in the U.S. in 2017.[21] A large percentage of these people come to the U.S. to preserve their lives. Gang violence and government corruption are most often the reason for their escape. And yet, many who claim to be "pro-life", also advocate for sending these people back to their hopeless, violent communities where many will die, including children. To make it even more egregious, many of these immigration policies also apply to those who have lived in the U.S. for years.

Poverty – One of the leading reasons women give for having an abortion is that they cannot afford to have a child.[22] There are currently 11.9 million children in the U.S. who are impoverished[23] and 2.5 million children who are homeless.[24] If only religious people were as passionate about helping these children as they are about bringing more into the world.

Many other categories overlap with the pro-life issue. Outside of adoption, immigration, and poverty, pro-life issues also affect health care, education, economics, the death penalty, gun violence, war, and even racism. The problem is that many "pro-lifers" support party beliefs that diminish life in each of these areas, instead of promoting them.

Perhaps the most egregious hypocrisy of it all is that more than half of all abortions are performed on Christian women.[25] It is statistics like this that demonstrate that we must take a humbler approach to the issue of abortion. It also demonstrates that some are not willing to take their own advice and live by the same moral standards that they so vocally force upon others. It is issues like this that contribute to the overall hypocrisy of evangelicals within Western culture.

Part of the reason for this is the shame that many religious women feel when becoming pregnant out of wedlock. The shame is often a product of the church's teaching on sexuality. It is, of course, easier for men to get away with the consequences of pre-marital sex than it is for women who have to deal with all of the consequences that may occur as a result. Moreover, men are both the perpetrators of a bad doctrine of sexuality as well, as the prosecutors for those who may become pregnant.

However, there is something even more important that this statistic illustrates. Namely, there is a person behind every decision to have an abortion. There is a story. There are various reasons why a woman will seek out an abortion. Many times, the decision, the procedure, and the fallout are life-changing. The last thing a woman needs is to feel alone and judged during this time. We must care at least as much for the mother going through this experience as we do for the unborn.

For someone to claim they are pro-life means they don't cherry-pick which lives they think are worthy and, instead, they care for *all* innocent life. That starts by supporting policies that reduce abortions and provide a higher quality of life for children born in this country regardless of their creed or color.

Toward a Theology of Sexuality

The issue of human sexuality is complicated. Many theologians are hesitant to extend theology into the area of sexuality even though it is one of the most significant issues in culture and is even discussed in Scripture.

Perhaps the most important thing to understand about sexuality in the Greco-Roman culture is that it was vastly different from how it exists in our society today. An example of this are customs regarding modesty. There was much less modesty in the Greco-Roman culture than exists today. Public baths, restrooms, and nudity, in general, were all very common for people during that time. Relationships were largely social constructs meant to pair people of the same social class together, usually for economic or political purposes. Sex within relationships – particularly marital relationships - was practiced largely to procreate. It was not uncommon for married men—especially those in the upper-class - to have multiple sexual partners. It was, however, much rarer for women to have multiple partners. By the 4th century CE much of these customs had changed.

Evangelicalism seems obsessed with sexuality, despite contributing very little in the way of a healthy theology of sexuality. Most within evangelicalism are just happy keeping their daughters chaste and their sons heterosexual. Camps still exist today that work to "rehab" those who claim to be gay, using so-called conversion therapy, which has been widely discredited as abusive by the medical community. Evangelical camps also exist with the main goal to encourage young girls to remain chaste and not to tempt their brothers in Christ. Purity rings are a common gift from evangelical fathers to their teenage daughters, which are supposed to help remind the young girl about her commitment to virginity until marriage.

Purity Culture

Evangelical attempts to establish a purity culture is perhaps the greatest mistake evangelicalism has made regarding sexuality. Purity culture started in the late 1980s and was spearheaded by Josh McDowell and his best-selling book *Why Wait?*[26] Sexual purity quickly became a primary focus for youth groups around the country. Josh McDowell was not the only perpetrator of purity culture. Joshua Harris published a best-selling book in 1997 called *I Kissed Dating Goodbye*. The purpose of this book was to essentially prepare young men and women for the subordinate roles they would play in marriage. Joshua Harris would eventually come out and apologize to the Christian community for how much his book hurt people.

Purity culture piggybacked off from the hyper-masculine authoritarianism that had been predominating the previous 20 years of church culture.[27] Purity culture was designed to condition young men and young women to begin settling into the complementarian roles that they would fulfill later in marriage. The idea was that men were the protectors of women and women were damsels in distress. It wasn't just their physical safety that women need-ed protection for, but also their sexual integrity. In doing this, Christian women's sexuality was snatched away from them and given to men to control. Manipulation and guilt were the primary weapons used to accomplish this. These methods demonstrated that Christian men viewed women as incom-petent to manage their own sexuality and make decisions regarding their own bodies.

Everything in purity culture hinges on the female's ability to maintain modesty. Since men are "unable" to control their sexual urges, women are responsible for making sure they are not tempting their brethren into sin with their feminine wiles. Ultimately, purity culture is not as much about controlling whether or not their young people are having sex, but in men's ability to control female sexuality.

This was not the same standard for young men. When young men participated in sexual practices they were deemed as simply making a mistake. However, if a woman participated in the same acts, her virtue was put in question and her "mistake" could result in pregnancy. Purity culture strives to make sure that men receive virtuous women as wives.

Like many issues of sexuality within evangelicalism, purity culture was not biblically supported. Instead, it was based on generic passages that talk about "sexual immorality" in general. The unspecific nature of the passages weren't obvious to many because they had been culturally conditioned within the church to think of sex outside of marriage as wrong. However, there are no passages in Scripture that actually discuss this issue, and there is no science that backs up a theory that sex outside of marriage is unhealthy.

With that said, contrary to how our "secular culture" portrays sex, there is a sacredness to it. The Bible is unequivocal about this. Sex is not just a physical activity between two people but can also be spiritual and poetic. Sex is not something that should bring about shame. However, it is also not something that should be practiced indiscriminately. It is the most intimate act between human beings.

LGBTQ+

When I fell in love with my wife, it was mostly out of my control. I couldn't control most of the emotions I had for her, nor could I control the physiological effects she had on me. I had anxiety whenever we were apart. I was in love. Eventually, our love for each other led us to marriage. I did not make myself love her; I could not help but love her.

Sometimes people have the same feelings for those of the same sex. The feelings gay[28] couples have for each other are the same that heterosexual couples have. You cannot control who you fall in love with. And to think you can force someone not to love someone is beyond absurd – as anyone who has ever been in love will tell you. It took me a long time to wrap my head around this concept. I struggled to make the connection between, "I was born this way," which I always assumed was a genetic proclamation, and not being able to choose who you fall in love with.

Gay couples face numerous roadblocks in how they can express that love for one another. Restrictions on marriage used to (and in some places still do) limit legal recognition of gay couples, as well as the ability to share health insurance and be their partner's next of kin. There have been two notable improvements in this area in the latest decade in the U.S. First, the U.S. Supreme Court ruled in Obergefell v Hodges (2015) that states are required to allow and recognize same-sex marriages. Second, public opinion has largely tilted in support of these rights. According to the latest Gallup Poll on this subject, 71% of U.S. adults now support same-sex marriage.[29]

Despite this progress, religious fundamentalism continues its misguided and abusive crusade to "straighten out" non-heteronormative people. Individuals raised in these communities often stay "closeted" for fear of reprisal or due to the intense shame they feel. Suicide attempts occur four times the rate among LGBTQ+ youth than among heterosexual youth.[30] In fact, LGBTQ+ youth who experience minority stress, including physical violence, discrimination, housing instability, and attempts by their parents to change their sexuality, are 12 times more likely to attempt suicide than youth who did not experience these.[31]

It is important to understand that there are two sides to this issue. There is what I refer to as the secular side because it involves political, psychological, biological, and sociological factors. There is also a religious side, which deals with the theological and ethical implications of approving of said behavior. We will discuss both in depth in the next section.

The Secular and Religious Separation[32]

Many evangelicals confuse the secular issues related to same-sex rights with the religious ones. They don't realize that they don't have to agree with homosexual behavior to understand that, as American citizens, same-sex couples are entitled to the same benefits as heterosexual couples. However, since evangelicals often conflate the religious with the political, it is not surprising that their efforts to limit the rights of same-sex couples continue to occur.

Evangelicals argue that marriage is a God-given right. Marriage in the U.S. is not a God-given right; it is a legal right. That legal right comes with a host of privileges that are important for day-to-day health and wellbeing. If evangelicals' only concern is really with the sanctity of marriage, then perhaps we should detach all legal benefits that come with marriage and attach them to a separate legal mechanism. (My guess is that they wouldn't like that either.)

The objection to homosexuality on religious grounds revolves around a handful of passages in the Bible that, when taken together, appear to create an argument against homosexual behavior. The most popular story that seems to clearly undermine an affirming perspective is the story of Sodom and Gomorrah. In the story, which is told in Genesis 18-19, Lot is visited by two angels. The Sodomites threaten to gang rape the two men. Later in the story, God destroys the city because of their wickedness. This story has always been used as a "clobber passage" to demonstrate God's wrath towards homosexual behavior. If all we did was look at this passage in isolation and didn't expand outward to see the larger context, then maybe this passage would appear to condemn homosexual behavior. However, it is our task to be more interested in the truth of the passage than in what some people want it to say.

Ezekiel provides some clarity on this issue:

Now this was the sin of your sister Sodom: She and her daughters were arrogant, overfed, and unconcerned; they did not help the poor and needy. They were haughty and did detestable things before me. Therefore, I did away with them as you have seen. (Ezekiel 16:49-50)

According to Ezekiel, God's wrath was applied to something very different than what is often the common understanding of the story. God destroyed the cities because of their arrogance and lack of concern for the social needs of their community.

Leviticus 18:22 and 20:13 are often combined with the aforementioned story. These verses both prohibit homosexuality/bisexuality among men. However, these passages have a unique context to them. The clue to their understanding is in the specific mention of men. Why were women excluded from this "abomination"? These verses are referring to a very specific act known as *pederasty*. This was a common practice whereby men would have sexual relations with teenage boys. It was a rite of passage in some cultures.[33] Moreover, the abomination is not directed toward the two being male, but specifically towards pedophilia.

Perhaps the most compelling passage against homosexual behavior is Romans 1:26–27:

Because of this, God gave them over to shameful lusts. Even their women exchanged natural sexual relations for unnatural ones. In the same way, the men also abandoned natural relations with women and were inflamed with lust for one another. Men committed shameful acts with other men and received in themselves the due penalty for their error.

The first thing to keep in mind is that homosexuality was a different cultural practice in ancient times than it is today. The practice of homosexuality was more of a casual sexual activity during the time Romans was written[34] rather than an act between two adults in a committed relationship. Therefore, as author Matthew Vines rightly points out:

> . . . same-sex relations in the first century were not thought to be the expression of an exclusive sexual orientation. They were widely understood to be a product of excessive sexual desire in general . . . It was a reflection of widespread cultural practices that differ greatly from modern ones.[35]

What Matthew asserts here is true. Paul's primary concern was sexual excess. It is important to note here that the people participating in these acts were bisexual. Their bisexual activity was seen as an excess outside of their normative heterosexual relationships. Furthermore, Paul's condemnation is not against committed, same-sex couples. We can infer this because during this time committed same-sex couples (as we see them in our society) were not as common as was bisexual behavior.

What is most concerning about this passage is Paul's assertion that this activity is "unnatural". Many have pointed to this word as the biggest hindrance for them to be affirming. Matthew Vines, along with others, argues that the term is about gender roles and not specifically homosexual behavior. Women were viewed in that time as inferior to men and homosexuality required one participant to take the sexually submissive role that was normally assumed by the woman. Therefore, the act was considered "unnatural".[36] There is a historical precedent to back up Vine's argument. Plato, Josephus, and Philo, among others, use the exact same language as Paul and they are much clearer about the word's application to gender roles.[37] Regardless of how one interprets the word "unnatural," it is clear that Paul is not referring to same-sex couples who are in committed relationships.

All people deserve to be treated with dignity and respect, regardless of their sexual orientation. When evangelicals strive to deny human rights to same-sex couples, they are saying one "sin" is greater than another. Their preoccupation with human sexuality is troublesome, not only because of the harm they do to the LGBTQ+ community, but also because it distracts them from caring for the needs of that community – ironically, the very thing that God condemned the Sodomites for.[38]

Racism, Immigration & Poverty

You may be wondering why topics like racism, immigration, and poverty are part of a book on theology. I admit that these issues are *not* theological in nature; they are largely political. However, they are important issues for the Church, especially among progressive Christians. These issues are to progressives what the "pro-life" movement is to evangelicals.

At first sight, the three chosen topics may appear to be random issues related to social justice, but in fact, they are all intimately connected. For example, immigration policy—or perhaps the lack of policy - throughout America's history has been largely dictated by racist agendas. In the early days of America, there were discriminatory policies against the Irish, Scottish, Africans, Germans, Mexicans, Chinese, etc. Many of those policies (such as indentured servitude) were eventually abolished but persisted for many years.

Racism is the fundamental issue that not only drives discriminatory immigration policies but also contributes to our nation's poverty. One could add a whole host of issues that are derivative of racism, such as disparities in education, inequality in vocational opportunities, and discrimination from law enforcement. The most significant barrier to overcoming racism in our country is what should be racism's biggest opponent - the Church, specifically, conservative evangelicalism.

As an example, conservative evangelicals have a history of hindering progress toward the equitable treatment of African Americans—from supporting slavery to opposition toward the Civil Rights movement. Even today, many conservative evangelicals deny there is even a problem with racism in this country.[39] Think about that for a minute. You have a group claiming they have been treated unfairly due to their race. Who is best equipped to assess whether this is true? The pale-skinned folks who benefit the most from this racial inequality or the people who are targeted by it?

Part of the problem is that many white people don't listen! They want to be in charge of the conversation. They want the conversation to be on their terms because they are used to being in a position of power. Instead of listening to what it's like to be a person of color in this country, they prefer to further perpetuate the problem by assuming they know better.

I admit that these issues are not limited to conservative evangelicals only; however, the complicity among Christian groups, is particularly acute. It is difficult for evangelicals, in particular, to see past any issue that is remotely political and to place it aside for the greater good. In the world of evangelicalism, politics oftentimes trumps God.

We need to understand that many policies are connected to the core ethical issues that the Church has been commanded by Jesus to address. Policies are not created in a vacuum. There must be accountability for how they are created, as well as an awareness of how they affect the lives of our neighbors. The Church should do what Jesus commands without making excuses. We should feed the poor—even if it's illegal. We should take care of immigrants—even if it's illegal. We should keep in mind that we are, first and foremost, Christians and not Republicans or Democrats.

Being & the Christian Life

Faith deconstruction is a scary and challenging journey. However, for those that persevere, they reach a point when they are ready to ask questions about what their faith should look like moving forward. Here the challenge becomes restructuring one's faith into something they can call their own.

We will cover this more in-depth in the Postscript, but this section explores the fundamental question of what it means to be a Christian. Does it mean that a person believes a set of propositions that were handed down to them from some faith tradition? And for those of us who have made the journey through reconstruction, what does that look like in for us today?

This book carefully examines multiple theological aspects of the Christian faith—both from evangelical and progressive viewpoints. This last chapter offers some final reflections for those on their deconstruction and reconstruction journey. Wherever you're at in your faith journey, I hope you'll live fully with the knowledge that you have something unique and important to offer the world, right where you are.

Some Christians struggle to understand their place and importance in this world. They see the world's problems as too big and themselves as too small or perhaps, even insignificant. Many of these people can get stuck—simply existing in the world, but not living purposefully in it. We don't stumble into our faith by accident. Christians have a calling to be a certain way in the world. There is meaning and purpose in our choice of being a Christian.

It takes courage to live purposefully in this world. The world is a hard place, full of difficult circumstances and people. Thankfully, it is not our responsibility to speak on behalf of God. We can only point others towards God so they can discern his voice for themselves. It is also not our responsibility to change the whole world. Instead, it is our job to change *our* world. All of us have something important to contribute to our own world of influence. Our goal should be to always leave a piece of ourselves with those we encounter. When we live this way our sphere of influence grows.

We have Jesus to thank for this framework. Jesus invested his time in many people - some apostles and many who were just normal people. Jesus's being was so significant that people never forgot when they encountered him. We are given an example of this in the story of the transfiguration in Matthew 17:1-11. In this story, we learn the transformative power of prayer as Jesus leaves his time with the father changed. His being radiated like a bright light. This type of restorative regeneration is available to all of us. To be clear, the transfiguration demonstrated the *divine* nature of Jesus, but we cannot help but look with hope at his example. Our lives as Christians involve both a personal relationship to God and divinely-inspired actions that change who we are.

Martin Heidegger, the well-known existential philosopher, had a term for the way of life that Jesus modeled. In his work *Being and Time*,[40] Heidegger coined the concept *Dasein* or "being-in-the-world". Heidegger describes *Dasein* as an obligation that the individual has to live with a highly meaningful orientation. He argues that all humans are interconnected and each has a destiny to fulfill. People who take *Dasein* seriously understand their being as significant and they act upon that understanding, which will inevitably inspire others to do the same. This is our responsibility to ourselves, to humanity—and I would also argue—to God.

Properly existing in the world means you're willing to take risks so that your life can benefit from the outcome; that you are willing to make your voice be heard because your opinion matters and reflects who you are; that you are willing to stand apart from the crowd.

Many people in this world are willing to settle for contentment as their end goal. A person who decides to exist properly in the world will not settle for contentment. Being content is safe. There is no risk involved. Taking risks is always uncomfortable, but it can lead to the greatest moments in life. After all, God did not call us to be safe and comfortable, but rather to live meaningful and thoughtful lives.

Ultimately, existing properly in this world means that we are always present to ourselves and our context, that we are in a perpetual state of awareness both of ourselves and others. Being present makes meaning possible because it is intentional—it has purpose. This self-awareness allows us to be in a constant state of reflectiveness. Being reflective helps mitigate destructive thinking, beliefs, and behaviors. This mitigation occurs because we are more aware of our self's impetus towards certain behaviors.

Our state of being and the motivations we have towards the world should be colored by our faith. When we say we are going to be like Christ,[41] what we are essentially saying is that we are allowing our identity to be subsumed by his. Many are under the assumption that being a Christian means holding certain beliefs and convictions. Christianity does indeed involve specific beliefs, but those beliefs alone are not what defines someone as a Christian. When a Christian "shares" Jesus with others, they often attempt to transfer their beliefs and convictions onto the other person (whether they want it or not). When they do this, they ignore the larger calling of being. Being-in-the-world requires a sense of presence that allows the Christian to sense the need the other individual has. The Christian should seek to present Christ in the context of that need. Providing for these needs is always the starting point for developing a relationship whereby the Christian can radiate Christ-likeness to the other. This is why being is so important. Ultimately, it is the Christian's being that will be the witness to the hope of Christ.

Much like the religious leaders of Jesus's day, evangelicals take a cognitive approach to evangelism. They believe that a person becomes a Christian when they accept some basic propositions about Christianity to be true. However, Jesus confronted this cognitive approach used by the religious leaders of his time. The religious leaders constantly challenged the teachings of Jesus, and he almost always rebutted them with follow-up questions about their own behaviors. In Matthew 23:1–4 Jesus addresses this while preaching to a crowd that had gathered.

Then Jesus said to the crowds and to his disciples:

> The teachers of the law and the Pharisees sit in Moses' seat. So,
> you must be careful to do everything they tell you. But do not
> do what they do, for they do not practice what they preach.

Jesus was not crucified for what he believed—that was just the legal excuse given. Jesus was crucified for what he represented in the world. Jesus never implored us to *believe* a certain way. He always directed us to *be* a certain way. He never told his disciples that following a list of rules is what makes you a follower of his. Instead, he said to love your neighbor, worship God, and share the hope that I give the world. He said, "Be like me."

CHRISTIANITY WILL ALWAYS BE necessary because there will always be people in need—a need for help, a need of relationships, a need of love and compassion; a need for hope! Until we die or Christ returns (or the zombie apocalypse occurs), Christianity will always be needed regardless of its relevance within the community. However, it is our job to maintain that relevance within the community because of the trust that it builds.

Over the last 20 years, the Church—particularly the conservative side - has diminished its relevance within the world. Many do not have any desire whatsoever for the Church because of the behaviors and practices of the conservative branch of Christianity. Relevance is important because Christians want others to see their need for God. We want our testimony to matter. We want our word to mean something. We want others to trust that we truly care for them without an agenda.

Without relevance who is there to love their neighbor when everyone else has abandoned them? Where is an understanding shoulder for tears? Who is there to provide hope for the brokenhearted? Jesus did all of these things when he lived. We are called to follow his steps, imitating what has been put on display for us.

In order to do this, we must remain relevant to our culture. We must be able to adapt the Gospel to an ever-changing world that is largely hopeless. We must not just bring Jesus to them; we must *be* Jesus for them. That is the calling of every Christian—to be Jesus. That is how we will remain relevant.

DISCUSSION QUESTIONS

1. What is the purpose of the Church?

2. What does it mean to be a Christian?

3. Do you believe in Hell? If so, do you believe that Hell is eternal?

4. What do you think about the role of women in the Church? Should there be any distinction between men and women in ministry?

5. Do you think the Bible condemns same-sex marriage? What convinces you of this conviction?

8

POSTSCRIPT

*"When you forgive somebody, when you are generous, when you
withhold judgment, when you love and when you stand up to
injustice, you are, in that moment, bringing heaven to earth."*
— **Rob Bell**

*"One of the most destructive mistakes we Christians make is to
prioritize shared beliefs over shared relationship, which is deeply
ironic considering we worship a God who would rather die than
lose relationship with us."*
— **Rachel Held Evans**

THIS BOOK IS A guide for the doubters, for those in the process of deconstructing and reconstructing their Christian faith. This final chapter offers a pathway for answering the question, "What now?" What follows is my guide to help deal with the psychological trauma that may result from the deconstruction/reconstruction process.

But first, I feel I should offer a trigger warning. The journey of looking inward is challenging. It forces us to confront difficult feelings about our faith tradition – and the people we share those traditions with. Some may find it useful to work through this chapter with a trusted friend or therapist.

Deconstruction requires the courage to critically think about one's faith regardless of where that path takes you. It is allowing the doubts you have been harboring deep in your mind to come to the surface. The aftermath of deconstruction can feel disorienting, like standing in front of your home that has just burned down. Reconstruction is the process by which you take the foundation you have, however unsteady, and decide what to build on top of it.

This book deconstructs many evangelical beliefs about Christianity and offers perspectives to aid in the reconstruction process. The tools I've offered here can help you understand your faith in a new way, but you are in control of your faith journey. It's no one's faith but your own. The work you put into this endeavor will determine what is built on your foundation.

This journey comes with sacrifice and pain. There is the pain of leaving the certainty of your old faith tradition and who you were within it, the shock of encountering a new God, and the relationships that may be broken in the process. This chapter is meant to provide support for those who struggle integrating this new kind of faith into their lives.

There are often psychological and emotional impacts from the journey of deconstruction and reconstruction. Some are good, but some can be traumatic. How can we heal from the past and move forward in our faith? What about the people who contributed to our former way of thinking? It is important to understand the art of healing and reconciliation – for our own wellbeing as well as those we love.

Knowing Who You Are

Reconciliation and healing begin with understanding who you are and who you want to be. Take time to do an honest survey of who you are and what you are feeling. Below is a list of questions you might reflect on:

- What matters most to me right now?

  - How can I engage in that more?

- Who are my support people?

- Do I carry any shame with me?

  - Shame is not from God. Cast it off and believe in it no more.

- What worries me right now?

  - What can I do to worry less?

- Am I happier now than I was before?

There is something about the process of self-examination that can lead to empowerment and optimism about the future. Here are some questions to consider about the future:

- What do I want to value in the future?

- What are some spiritual goals I have?

  - How can I achieve them?

- What is one bad habit I want to change?

  - How will I go about changing it?

- What do I want to start doing?

  ◦ What might prevent me from doing it?

- Who are some people I need to reconcile with?

These questions may not be easy, and you may benefit from professional help to guide you through answering some of them. This self-examination could also take some time to answer and that is okay. There is no timetable for reconstruction.

Many reach a point in their reconstruction journey when they ask the question, "Who do I need to reconcile with?" You may wonder what this has to do with spirituality. Emotional health is just as important to take care of as spiritual health. In fact, the two are inseparable. Deconstruction often results in tension and even animosity within families and faith communities who largely don't understand the value of the deconstruction process. The role of reconciliation acts to mitigate those feelings by helping to restore/repair broken relationships (where it is safe to do so).

One aspect of having and maintaining good emotional health during this process is to make sure you are not holding any animosity towards other people. Importantly, reconciliation *does not* require the other person to agree with your reconciliation effort. It may be the case that you have tried to reconcile with someone, and it doesn't work. All you can do is your part. You may notice a huge burden is released once you have attempted reconciliation. It can be difficult to clean away the rubble from deconstruction without coming to terms with the tension in some of your relationships. Full reconstruction means full restoration as a person who is capable of moving forward—to become whole again.

There are going to be people who oppose what you are doing and what you did. You will have to figure out how you are going to handle those individuals. It will be important for you to learn how to identify people and beliefs that are toxic. Toxic people and beliefs can undo some of the hard work you have put into your faith. Not all relationships can be reconciled and not all are worth reconciliation.

Some people will fear the changes you have made, especially if it appears you have lost your faith and/or abandoned your denomination or church. You will have to decide how forthcoming to be about your journey and with whom. I am reminded of this passage:

> But in your hearts revere Christ as Lord. Always be prepared to give an answer to everyone who asks you to give the reason for the hope that you have. But do this with gentleness and respect (1 Peter 3:15).

Some people will be confused by the joy that you have. This joy will be the result of the freedom you now feel to live your life for Christ and to enjoy the world at the same time. They may interpret the new freedom you feel as permitting yourself to sin. However, in reality, what is happening is that you are permitting yourself to live. There is nothing wrong with enjoying the creation that God has made. What many Christians have failed to understand is that you can love the world without participating in unethical behavior. The world is not always bad.

It's Grief!

Grief is often associated with the loss of a loved one, but grief can manifest itself in many ways. Losing one's old way of life may cause grief. In fact, it would be surprising if it didn't. Grief affects everyone differently. One's level of grief will vary depending on how long someone is exposed to toxic religion or how much they "lost" during their deconstruction and reconstruction journey.

There is often nothing a person can do about grief except go through it. There are stages—or, more accurately, feelings that are dominant during certain times in the grieving process. Grieving well takes time. There is little that can be done to speed up that recovery process, although grief counseling or grief support groups can help people cope and accept their loss in time. Healing after loss is usually slower than we would like but recognizing the stages one is going through can be helpful. Below are four stages of spiritual grief that I have adapted from the general five stages of grief that are more commonly known.

1. **Denial/Shock** – It is not always obvious who or what the culprit of your grief is. If it is someone close to you, it can be difficult to admit that this person is responsible for some of your pain—especially if it is someone you care about or put your trust in (e.g., a parent or a spiritual leader). This denial stage may be coupled with shock if one experiences unexpected loss of relationships due to deconstruction. The world may feel overwhelming, and you may feel helpless to change the circumstances. Oftentimes we attribute feelings of grief to things outside of what the actual cause is. Understanding the true cause, and coming to terms with it, is the key to moving forward.

2. **Anger** – Being angry is an important part of the healing process. It is important to feel your anger as well as properly identify the source of that anger. Is it a pastor, leader, the Church, God, etc.? Feeling your anger is what will give you the energy to enact positive change. Identifying what makes us angry can help us develop antithetical behaviors.

3. **Depression** – Emptiness, feelings of overwhelming sadness and withdrawal tend to be hallmarks of this stage. This is the stage where people most often leave church. There may be a time were leaving church is necessary. This is completely fine as long as you can identify the reason why you are leaving and reflect on how grief is manifesting in your life.

4. *Acceptance* – Accepting your situation and having a willingness to move forward is the final stage of spiritual grief. It may mean going back to church or opening yourself back up to relationships you had. It is important to understand that accepting something is not the same thing as being okay with whatever occurred. The key here is that you are taking back your life – taking control over your own faith. This is a good stage to develop a plan to return to church, if that's what you desire. There are many mainstream and progressive churches that may be a good choice while you are coming to terms with your new faith perspective.

It is important that we don't minimize our feelings by rationalizing them or tucking them away in the back of our minds. This will cause more damage to us in the future. Instead, we must deal with these feelings so that we can open ourselves back up to God and others.

Opening Ourselves Back Up

Many people who go through deconstruction experienced harm from those in the religious tradition they left. This harm can lead the newly deconstructed to cut ties with people with whom they have deep emotional ties – for better or worse. This separation is often necessary to give the individual time to process, deconstruct, reconstruct, and ultimately heal from their experiences. It may also be necessary to maintain this separation to avoid additional harm.

There is another consequence to this harmful past: It can be difficult to trust people when you've been hurt by those who are supposed to take care of you, teach you, and love you. When you've been burned, it's common to close yourself off to others.

There comes a point for most of us when we realize it is important to open ourselves back up to some people from our past religious tradition. Despite how difficult it might be or how afraid we are, the process of reconstruction typically involves some kind of reconciliation, although this is not always possible. Open and honest relationships, particularly with family members and friends who differ religiously, will inevitably bring some tension, conflict, and criticism. It is important to learn how to deal with that criticism in a healthy way that is productive for both parties.

Relentless criticism is what often drives people away from the faith. It is always important to remember that the Church and its people are not God. People are fallible and all relationships take effort. With that said, an individual should *never* remain in a toxic relationship simply for the sake of preserving some religious ideal. It takes two people to have a relationship and if the other person is not willing to do their part to make the relationship healthy, then there is nothing they can do.

It is important to keep in mind that while the road to reconciliation is often difficult, the burden of carrying unresolved conflict is also a heavy burden to bear. Reconciliation can bring healing to an individual that is necessary for them to move forward in their lives. After all, humans are relational beings. Relationships are necessary for thriving in this world and - for the Christian - for advancing the Kingdom of God.

However, we are not the same as we were before our deconstruction and reconstruction. We have to learn to find our voice again or find it for the first time with a liberated view of the world. Either way, it is important to speak – to make yourself heard. You have important things to say and contribute to the Church – regardless of who you are. Confidence in your faith is often an outcome of the reconstruction journey. Many people are not confident in their original faith tradition because it was handed to them. When you have done the work to develop your own faith, you can feel more confident in this part of your life.

Spiritual Identity

Many people who have been indoctrinated into a particular faith tradition usually reach a point when they start to doubt the tenants of that tradition. This most often occurs in young and early adulthood. Doubt is highly discouraged in fundamentalist religious environments, or as I like to call them, cults. Doubt is healthy and necessary as is critical thinking. It is important to maintain a balance between learning and acceptance. There is a difference between learning new information and accepting that information as true. Critical thinking is a habit that we cannot afford to live without.

After deconstruction and reconstruction, some people find they need reconcile with their pastor, especially if they still want to attend the same church. Still other people will look for a new place to worship that a better fit for their new perspective on faith. Whatever church you are a part of, make sure you find leaders that you can trust. One way this can happen is through conversation. Interview a new pastor to see what impressions you get from them. You will have a new sense of awareness after you reconstruct your faith, you can utilize that to see what your "Spidey sense" tells you.

Learning From Our Past, Living for Our Future

Shame is not from God. I am reminded of Romans 10:11. "As Scripture says, 'Anyone who believes in him will never be put to shame.'" Shaming people is a common tactic used in fundamentalist religious environments to promote strict compliance with the rules of the group. Those coming out of these environments may still carry some of that shame. Your past will always exist in the rearview mirror. It will always be present, so to speak, but you don't need to live there. You are greater than the sum of your parts. You can choose to make a change at any time – to move the trajectory from where you came from toward a new future of your own making. Reconstruction is a journey without a destination. You are always adding on top of the new faith you reconstructed. You are "working out your salvation with fear and trembling."[1]

Narrative Identity

The process of deconstruction and reconstruction can be transformative for individuals brave enough to put in the time and effort. Evangelicals use the phrase "born again" to refer to when the Christian life begins for an individual and their identity shifts to something new. Well, deconstruction and reconstruction are the progressive Christian equivalent to being born again. Individuals can begin their faith anew on better terms, where the Jesus of the Bible is actually worshipped vs. the white-washed caricature embraced by evangelicals.

Narrative identity is the idea that our lives tell a story, and that story has a profound impact on who we are. Narrative identity can help us understand the purposes of our past and give us hope for our future. Narrative identity is not just the ability to construct our own story, but it allows us to see how our story fits into the larger metanarrative that God is writing throughout history.

In order for us to understand how this narrative forms, it is important to understand how we influence others and how they influence us. We need to recognize that "significance" in the Kingdom is much different than it is in society. We don't need to be "famous" to have significance. We are the kings and queens of our own world. Our world is often defined by those who surround us – those who we encounter by accident or on purpose. We are called to be influencers within our world. For some that world expands given the type of influence we provide. Some of us are a part of smaller worlds, but we are all a part of a world, and we all have influence over that world.

We must understand that our faith journey up to this point was no accident—no misstep. For reasons only known to God, our journey up to this point had a purpose, even if we are unsure as to what that purpose was. Looking to our past through a positive lens rather than a negative one will help us to better accept what we have experienced. Those experiences have shaped our "narrative identity". It is a part of our story, and we are a part of God's story.

Narrative identity is about allowing us, through the help of God, to write our own story. Far too often we give that right to other people. We allow our religious leaders, our politicians, our family, and our friends to dictate to us how our story should go. To be in charge of our own life is to have the ability to write our own chapters and to live on our own terms.

Therefore, we must look to the future with hope and not disdain or fear. Believe it or not, we can control much of our future. We do encounter unexpected events, but it is the shape of our identity which dictates how we will deal with those unexpected events. We have two options when it comes to our future, we can sit back and let it come to us, which will require that living reactionary lives, or we can be proactive about our future by taking each step with intention and purpose.

Being proactive about your future is the only way you can control what your narrative is. It is the only way you can control the legacy you strive to leave. All of our stories are unique, and our desire should be the legacy our stories leave. What type of influence did we have over our worlds and what will minstrels sing about us after our stories end?

I USE THE PROGRESSIVE Christianity platform not because there is necessarily a central belief system that I adhere to. Instead, I use progressive Christianity as a means to an end. It serves as a safe place where I have been able to deconstruct and reconstruct my faith. I have learned a lot from my fellow sojourners who have accompanied me through my transitions. I have included many of those voices within this book.

I wish evangelicals and other conservative groups understood that progressive Christianity would not be necessary if they followed the ministry of Jesus and modeled his tolerance of doubt and disillusionment. Progressive Christianity wouldn't be needed if evangelicals took responsibility for the actions of their past and present that have and continue to hurt people. I wish progressive Christianity wasn't necessary, but it is. Thank God for it, as it continues to be a refuge for those who wander.

I desire that this little book will give people hope; that it will be a tool for those who feel lost. Hopefully, this book will also provide a foundation for readers to research more on their own – and to know how to do that. Ultimately, I desire that the reader has learned how to ask good questions of their faith and critically think about the doctrine that accompanies it.

May the Lord bless and keep you in his arms as you live your new life of faith.

Amen!

APPENDIX A

NARRATIVE PERSPECTIVISM: AN INTRODUCTION

THIS IS A VERY brief description of Narrative Perspectivism. This "perspective" is still in its infancy stages. The purpose of including it here is to provide a resource for those who desire to have a framework for interpreting Scripture. I hope that others who read this can build upon it as well. In the technological sense, we can think of this as open-source theology.

If UNenlightening ourselves has taught us anything about theology, it's that "methods" have their place, but not in theology. Therefore, what I am proposing is changing our approach from "systematic methodologies" to "perspectives." This is a significant difference in approaching the biblical text. Methodologies force us to put an interpretive layer over the top of the text. This layer can oftentimes lead us to anachronistic readings of Scripture. Perspectives allow us to stand back and let the text come to us in all of its contextual glory.

Narrative Perspectivism's approach is philosophical, theological, and literary. These three components allow for the breadth of Scripture to be captured in a way that is faithful to the various textual genres, as well as the humanity contained therein (the characters) and outside (the author) of the text.

The Problem with Systemic Methods

Systematic Theology is built upon the premise that Modernity's absolutism is the correct lens through which we can and should understand reality. At the heart of absolutism is the denial of metaphysics, which is ultimately the mythical conjecture of ideas. Modernity's framework has served systematic theology well since most of those who employ that methodology (most evangelicals and mainline Protestants) are absolutists. The absurdity of using objective, physical systems to relay truths about metaphysical reality is mind-boggling to me.

In addition to the ontological consequences previously mentioned, there are also biblical consequences. Systematic theology almost demands a propositional-based theological structure. The task of systematic theology is to create an organizational method for bringing together various biblical propositions. It's not a far leap from employing one's propositions within their theological locus to proof-texting. In other words, because the propositions already exist, it's easy to appeal to them when having to defend one's theological position.

Methods are devoid of personalization and imagination. That is, methods abstract propositional content in order to determine meaning. If we were merely dealing with a text that was devoid of personal content and idiosyncrasies, then we might be able to apply a systematic method to the interpretive framework. However, the Bible consists of both formal and informal forms of literature that require a "person," not a "method" to understand what it is saying.

For example, there is no method for reading a letter. Sure, there might be some rules for writing a letter, but most people just write what they are thinking and don't care about formalities. The majority of the New Testament are letters. They were not written by their authors with the intent that one day they might be a part of Scripture. Certainly, the New Testament writers did not think their letters were on par with what the prophets wrote. Had the writers thought what they were writing would one day become a part of Scripture, they would have written them much differently.[1]

Scripture comprises a wide variety of literary forms: history, myths, songs, poetry, apocalyptic, personal correspondence, and biography. It is illogical to try and interpret this large arch of literature with a single "method;" however, this is exactly what is taught in most seminaries and widely practiced in a majority of Christian churches. For example, this systematic approach to the Bible is the main reason why creationist interpretations of Scripture exist. Creationists look at a myth and interpret it literally – despite the overwhelming scientific and historical evidence to the contrary. This happens because they are using the same interpretive framework for Genesis as they do for any other type of book.

If we truly trust Scripture to speak truth to us, then we must be bold enough to allow it to speak to us on its own terms instead of forcing it to say certain things. Narrative Perspectivism restores our confidence in the interpretive process by allowing Scripture to speak organically.

Perspectives Over Systems

Systems provide a set of rules for the reader to use while engaging the biblical text. Perspectives acknowledge the reader's distance from the ancient text and provide ways the reader can understand that text regardless of how far they are from the source. In other words, systems always start with the now and then move's back towards the text; whereas perspectivism begins with the text and moves forward.

To be fair a systematic theologian might argue that the methods they employ are just contemporary tools meant to better understand the text as it was written. And that their organizational methods only exist as a way to create coherence for a bunch of ancient documents spread over a thousand years. However, what many of these theologians fail to acknowledge is that just because we are reading an ancient text in a more technologically sophisticated time period, which does not mean that our "tools" are more sophisticated than those the writers employed two thousand years ago. If we ever want to understand what it was an ancient writer was trying to say, we must "UNenlighten" ourselves of that which only serves as contemporary baggage that we bring to the biblical text.

What is Narrative Perspectivism

There are two core values to narrative perspectivism. The first is the understanding that Scripture and history intersect within what is called the metanarrative. That is, there is an overarching story that is taking place and at various points of that story, God interacts. God is the author of this metanarrative and sometimes makes a guest appearance which is testified to in the Bible – most dramatically as the "son," Jesus. Much of evangelical theology will acknowledge this aspect – though this is a more recent phenomenon. However, it is the second part of narrative perspectivism that often gets overlooked – perspective.

The Bible is a compilation of various types of literature. Much of this literature consists of poetic, musical, biographical, testimonial, correspondence, and mythical. There are various perspectives in Scripture. There is first person, second person, and third person. For any work of literature, this would be enough for perspective to be fully represented. However, what makes Scripture different is the added fourth perspective. The voice of Scripture communicates not just to the characters within the story, but those characters that transcend the story – like those reading the story. This means our task of interpretation has become a little more difficult, but also a little more exciting because when we interpret Scripture, we become part of it. We are the fourth-person perspective that Scripture speaks to.

Scripture not only tells a story, but it also speaks to us on a personal level because we believe that God is involved in some way. God transcends the story because ultimately, he is its author. And we can become a part of the story because ultimately God is in control of history.

Presuppositional Perspectives

Everything within Scripture resembles a literary framework. There exist characters, narrators, writers, and a divine voice. These characters are broken down into personal perspectives (i.e., first, second, and third-person perspectives). Understanding the perspective of the author and the characters helps create a depth that is missing in contemporary theological methods.

There should be very little difference between what something means and how that meaning is applied. The more space we create between meaning and application the greater the chance we have for misapplying and therefore, misunderstanding the purpose of a given text.

The Concentric Circles of Context

The only way to understand what the Bible is trying to communicate is to understand how context works. The more context that is exposed, the deeper one's understanding of a particular passage is. This context emanates out of the text and allows us to jump into the world the writer is from so that we can better understand what is being said. When we jump into the author's world we can look around and ask the question, what do we see? This is a different position than the systematic theologian who will simply ask what does the text shows us. Therefore, there is a differentiation between observing just the text and the world that the author exists within.

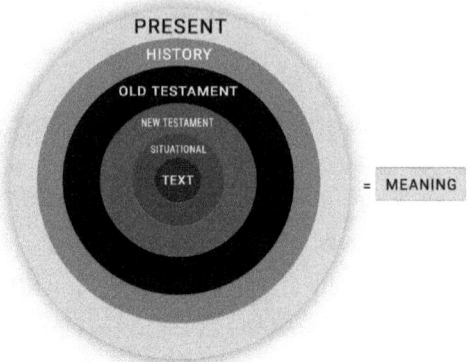

We will break down each contextual component, but let's first take a moment to define each of the areas. The first concentric circle is the situational context. This is all of the immediate context associated with the passage under consideration. This includes cultural-linguistic context. Assuming the passage under consideration is from the New Testament, the second concentric circle asks the question what does the situational context mean in light of the New Testament Context? This includes a larger look at the cultural-linguistic milieu. As we continue to move outward, we include the Hebrew Scriptures for context and ask the question, "Does this passage require an understanding of some larger cultural-linguistic understanding? If so, what parts of the Hebrew Scriptures require this understanding?" The next section asks to what extent has church history/history commented on what is being said. This will help to determine whether or not a text is cultural or universal in its application. The final circle asks the metanarrative question, what does this mean in light of my situation?

Situational Context

The situational context is the foundation for whatever the text under consideration is. There is a reason why everything in Scripture is written. The situational context asks the question, what is the situation under which the text was written? This phase often requires the most research but having a good research Bible is handy for this part (not a Life Application Bible, which forces conclusions based upon systematic methods).

As we begin to move higher and higher, lifting the lens on the passage, we begin to ask different questions. This part also requires that we understand the type of literature that is being employed. Is it a narrative, a prophetic book, a letter, etc.? What is the situation(s) the author is addressing; there is always a situation.

New and Old Testament Context

As our view increases, so does our perspective. It is in this phase that we ask the question of a larger historical context, keeping in mind the cultural-linguistic signatures that will give us hints into how we should understand the passage. The Hebrew Scriptures always act as the context for the New Testament regardless of what text is being read. Whether that is a tradition or a direct quote, every writer brings the Hebrew Scriptures with them when they write.

For example, we might ask what are the presuppositions the author has? If it is a New Testament passage, we might wonder whether context from the Hebrew Scriptures helps us to better understand the passage. If it is a passage out of the Hebrew Scriptures, we may have to appeal more to secular sources, such as archeology, anthropology, etc., to help us better understand what is being said in the greater Ancient Near East culture.

However, when we appeal to historical (secular) sources, we must do so carefully. We must compare multiple sources to ensure that what one source says is accurate. Although history is supposed to be a scientific endeavor, there is still room for interpretation and that is where you can get into trouble when sourcing your material.

Church History Context

For better or worse the Church Fathers have created much of the Christian faith that exists today. Their toil and insight created the orthodoxy that many of us adhere to. Their insights are especially valuable because they were intellectuals who knew much about the culture that we are too far removed from to understand. For example, many of them wrote under persecution or in the same domineering Roman society that the New Testament authors also wrote from. Some of them were even connected to the disciples indirectly and only removed by a few generations.

The question that we want to ask of these great Patriarchs is what was their understanding of the passage or idea is and why? It is here where we might find a bias or interesting insights into the passage that we are looking into. Regardless, the goal is to trace throughout church history to see how the belief has developed over time until it gets us to our present context.

Present Context and Application

The question of present context asks if the belief or idea is understood similarly or differently than it would have been at the time it was written and/or in church history.

For example, if we chose the issue of "women in ministry" and read all of the passages that seem to discourage women from participating in ministry, then we would have to ask the question, "Are there any contextual differences between the New Testament and the present?" The answer, of course, is a resounding "yes." First of all, the New Testament culture was still largely agrarian, whereas today many of us are reading this in a culture where intellect is the highest capital. Could those differences be enough to account for the difference in context? Yes. In fact, they are the primary reason the texts regarding women in ministry are cultural and not universal axioms.

The question to present context is really a question about the application. However, what we are doing during our application phase is determining whether or not the biblical command is universal or cultural. If universal, then there is no choice, but to believe it. The only possible way to dispute the passage is to make sure that it has been interpreted correctly to begin with. This is accomplished through the church history phase. Otherwise, the passage is cultural and can have a new interpretation in the reader's present situation.

Meaning

Although you can attempt to capture the meaning of a text at any stage of the process. It is only truly found after all contextual factors have been considered. Most people rarely get past the first or second circle – believing there is enough contextual clues in the text itself to determine its meaning. In fact, many pastors rarely get past the first few stages finding it cumbersome and unnecessary to move any further. However, if you want to fully understand the text you will need to pursue all of the stages.

Some might question whether it is really necessary to follow all of these stages in order to determine the truth of a passage. It is true that some passages may just be axiomatic. For example, it is not necessary to consult history in trying to understand why "Jesus wept." However, it is absolutely necessary to move at least through situational context and perhaps Old Testament context.

ALTHOUGH INCOMPLETE, I BELIEVE Narrative Perspectivism has great potential for biblical interpreters – especially for laypeople. It is a way that can allow the biblical text to speak to us without superimposing our perspective upon the text.

APPENDIX B

THE BIBLE IS NOT THE WORD OF GOD: A POLEMIC AGAINST CHRISTENDOM

This article was written and published on Patheos.com in 2013. It quickly became viral and acted as a catalyst for my personal reconstruction. I have included it in this book as an Appendix in order to promote further encouragement for believers every-where!

THE BIBLE IS NOT the word of God and if we believe it is then we have made the Bible into an idol.

The Bible is not the WORD OF GOD. And if we believe it as such, then we have made the Bible into an idol. The Bible has become the Church's idol. It is the Golden Calf of our day. The ancient Hebrews had taken the God of their forefathers and formed him into their image. They made him take on their identity because they could not grasp to what extent the WORD OF GOD was present with them. Yes, indeed it has been said for thousands of years that the ancient Hebrews were fools for doing so, but my dear friend so are we.

Just as the Hebrews, we have made the WORD OF GOD into our image—the Bible. And by doing so have not elevated God but relegated him to the lowliest place. Our misappropriation of authority has inevitably resulted in our inability to distinguish between what we *think* God requires of us, and what God *actually* requires of us. This misappropriation has resulted in our use of superfluous language.

The Bible is not the WORD OF GOD. However, our elevation of the Bible to almost divine status has seemingly resulted in the Church believing it is to be the moral authority over the world – as though they speak for God. We have equated the language of the Bible with the Words of God. This has seemingly resulted in the Bible being used as a weapon of power to oppress others. Incredibly, the Church's oppression has not been limited to the secular world but has even been used as a weapon to oppress its own people.

Jesus Never Oppressed Anyone!

When we assert that the Bible is the WORD OF GOD, we are diminishing what it means to possess the WORD OF GOD. The Bible is a book. Just like any other book, it contains words, propositions, stories, ideologies, and philosophies. But it contains something that is far greater than any other book that has ever been written. It contains testimonies. But not just any testimony. It contains testimonies about God – not just about any God, but the living God. It contains testimonies about who God is, and who man is; and who man is in light of his discovery of God.

God has revealed himself in history. Scripture testifies to that revelation. Scripture is not revelation in and of itself. Rather, it is a testimony to the revelation that has occurred. The Bible is what we learn from; it is what we abide by, and it is what strengthens our faith.

The Bible is not the WORD OF GOD. It has no special powers, and it is not magic. Sacred Scripture means nothing if it is not alive inside the individual. Embodied, fully embraced. This does not mean that we take apart or dissect the Bible in such a way that we can extrapolate metaphysical truths about the world around us. That is not the intent of the Bible. Rather, the intent of the Bible is to provide context for who we are as human beings, who God is as God; and how God has acted throughout history. It is a testimony to our Lord Jesus Christ.

The WORD OF GOD is a moment that a human being encounters. It is Jesus Christ in his full glory and revelation. The WORD OF GOD occurs through a compilation of acts that bring forth the WORD OF GOD within the individual—prayer, reading, and meditating on sacred Scripture, fellowship, and worship.

Encountering the WORD OF GOD changes us—it makes us whole. It gives us strength and power. Words on a page do not give us strength; they do not give us power. It is only when we embody those words on the page that we truly become like the WORD OF GOD. It is what Jesus did. He did not come to abolish the law but to fulfill it. That means he embodied the law. He was sinless, he was perfect. He embodied the law in the truest, purest form of what is meant by "the law." Likewise, we must embody Scripture. It must become a part of us, our lives, and our identity; for the truth of God was not found in words or propositions or abstract ideas, but in the truthfulness that exists when we live out the WORD OF GOD on the world stage.

The Bible is not the WORD OF GOD. The WORD OF GOD is Jesus Christ.

APPENDIX C

RESOURCES FOR DECONSTRUCTION / RECONSTRUCTION

HISTORICAL AUTHORS			
Title	Author	Difficulty	Description
Provocations	Soren Kierkegaard	9	A series of short essays that provoke deep thinking about Christianity.
The Essential Karl Barth	Keith Johnson	8	A reader and commentary on several of Barth's important ideas.
Church Dogmatics	Karl Barth	10	Barth's magnum opus that discusses "liberal" dogmatics in the Church.
Oneself as Another	Paul Ricoeur	9	A discussion on the nature of personal identity.
I see Satan Fall like Lightning	Rene Girard	9	Discusses why God appears to be violent and the nature of myth-making.
The Meaning of Revelation	H. Richard Niebuhr	7	Looks at how God reveals himself through a more progressive lens.

Scale 1-10 with 10 being the most difficult.

THEOLOGY			
Title	Author	Difficulty	Description
Jesus Unforsaken	Keith Giles	6	Helpful for understanding atonement theories more in-depth.
Reading the Bible Again for theFirst Time	Marcus Borg	6	How to approach the Bible after deconstruction.
Convictions	Marcus Borg	7	Addresses essential doctrinal issues.
How Not to Speak about God	Peter Rollins	6	An introduction to the philosophical issues related to postmodern/progressive Christianity.
Genesis for Normal People	Peter Enns	5	An easy-to-read commentary on the book of Genesis.
The Idolatry of God	Peter Enns	6	Breaking our addiction to certainty.
Love Wins	Rob Bell	5	Universalism, Heaven, and Hell.
The Very Good Gospel	Lisa Sharon Harper	5	How what is wrong can be made right.
Inspired	Rachel Held Evans	6	How we should approach the Bible.
Sinners in the Hands of a Loving God	Brian Zahnd	6	Questioning the wrath of God.
The Inescapable Love of God	Thomas Talbott	8	Eternal reconciliation

Scale 1-10 with 10 being the most difficult.

THE CHRISTIAN LIFE			
Title	Author	Difficulty	Description
Out of Sorts	Sarah Bessey	5	A deconstruction of the issues that we all go through.
Faith After Doubt	Brian McLaren	5	How to move forward after encountering doubt.
Life Together	Dietrich Bonhoeffer	5	Establishing Authentic Community.
Searching for God Knows What	Donald Miller	3	Faith in an ever-changing context.
A Church Called TOV	Scot McKnight	6	How to heal and move forward after a toxic church culture.
Jesus and John Wayne	Kristin Du Mez	6	A history of evangelicalism's political culture.
God and the Gay Christian	Matthew Vines	3	How to understand homosexuality while taking the Bible seriously.
I'm Still Here: Black Dignity in a World Made for Whiteness	Austin Channing Brown	3	Racism in the Church and racial justice.
Shameless	Nadia Bolz-Webber	4	Sexuality and gender.
Pure	Linda Kay Klein	4	Anyone who has suffered through purity culture.
The Reconstruction of your mind	Todd Vick	4	A post-deconstruction journey through issues of faith.

*Scale 1-10 with 10 being the most difficult.

END NOTES

INTRODUCTION

1. In other words, progressive Christianity is not the same thing as progressive liberalism.

2. Tony Jones, *The New Christians: Dispatches from the Emergent Frontier*. San Francisco: Jossey-Bass, 2008, 41.

3. The word "postmodern" was oftentimes used as a term of derision towards those within evan_ gelicalism. The primary reason was because evangelicals did not believe that Postmodernism had any real substance. Therefore, being called postmodern meant that you were a theological/philosophical lightweight.

4. Jeffrey Jones, "U.S. Church Membership Falls Below Majority for First Time." *Gallup.* March 29, 2021.

https://news.gallup.com/poll/341963/church-membership-falls-below-majority-first-time.aspx.

5. Ibid.

6. Speech-Act Theory was promoted by linguist J.L. Austin and philosopher Ludwig Wittgenstein. It was later popularized by Kevin Vanhoozer in the book *The Drama of Doctrine: A Canonical Linguistic Approach to Christian Theology* (Louisville, KY: Westminster John Knox Press, 2005).

CHAPTER ONE

1. Lindbeck. Lindbeck. *The Nature of Doctrine: Religion and Theology in a Postliberal Age*. London: Westminster John Knox Press, 1984, 20.

2. An important aspect to this conversation is the relationships presidents have had with these organizations, which have both sustained and progressed the indoctrination of these organizations. To read more about the relationship between these organizations and presidents, see Kristin Du Mez's work, Jesus and John Wayne: How White Evangelicals Corrupted a Faith and Fractured a Nation (New York, NY: Liveright, 2020). Du Mez traces this history on into the present and demonstrates why evangelicals overwhelmingly supported Donald Trump for president.

3. The exception to this is presuppositional apologetics, which is just an approved version of circular reasoning. That is, one is justified to believe in the idea of God apart from evidence as a premise from which they can create an argument. This a priori belief acts as both the presupposition, as well as the content yet to be proven (circular).

4. This is the conclusion of Alvin Plantinga's Reformed epistemology.

5. Pew Research Center. "Americans Express Increasingly Warm Feelings Toward Religious Groups." *Pew*. February 15, 2017. https://www.pewforum.org/2017/02/15/americans-express-increasingly-warm-feelings-toward-religious-groups/.

6. Kierkegaard, Soren. *Purity of Heart Is to Will One Thing*. New York: Harper Torchbooks, 1956, 185.

7. Whyte Jr., W.H. "Groupthink." *Fortune*. March 1952, 114–117, 142, 146. Whyte derived his idea of groupthink from George Orwell's book, *1984*.

8. Matthew 25.

9. Though one might argue that Thomas Aquinas also published a systematic theology which he called the *Summa Theologica*, (ed. Fathers of the English Dominican Province, New York: Benzinger Brothers, 1922).

10. Despite many of its benefits, Bible verses and chapter delineations have also resulted in the unfortunate growth of propositionalism.

11. McLaren, Brian. *Faith After Doubt: Why Your Beliefs Stopped Working and What To Do About It.* New York: St. Martin's Essentials, 2021, 113.

CHAPTER TWO

1. Borg, Marcus J. *Reading the Bible Again for the First Time: Taking the Bible Seriously but not Literally.* New York: HarperCollins, 2002, 3.

2. This book focuses on two groups within Protestant Christianity, so discussion of sexual abuse within the Catholic Church will not be discussed here, although I acknowledge the harm done within that part of the Church.

3. The Pseudepigrapha are the books that were written during the intertestamental period and are commonly included in the Catholic version of the Bible.

4. Borg, *Reading the Bible Again for the First Time,* 7.

5. A Christian theologian, a Church Father, and a noted Coptic Christian leader.

6. Schaff, Philip and Wace, Henry, eds. *Nicene and Post-Nicene Fathers, First Series, Vol. 3.* Buffalo: Christian Literature Publishing Co., 1892, 551.

7. Technically, the Vaticanus is older by roughly 30-50 years. However, this codex is different from the Bibles we possess today. Also, about half of the codex is missing.

8. A fifth century Christian manuscript of a Greek Bible, containing the majority of the Greek Old Testament and the Greek New Testament.

9. Grudem, Wayne A. *Systematic Theology: an Introduction to Biblical Doctrine.* Leicester: Inter-Varsity Press, 1994, 90.

10. A theologian, philosopher, and bishop whose most notable work, Confessions, was written between AD 397-400.

11. Woodbridge, John. "Did Fundamentalists Invent Inerrancy?" *The Gospel Coalition*. August 3, 2017. https://www.thegospelcoalition.org/article/did-fundamentalists-invent-inerrancy/.

12. Famous 15th- and 16th century Christian theologian, priest, author, composer, and former Augustinian monk, best known as a seminal figure in the Protestant Reformation and as the namesake of Lutheranism.

13. Lindbeck, *The Nature of Doctrine,* 16.

14. Ibid., 35.

15. A discourse between two or more people holding different points of view about a subject but wishing to establish the truth through reasoned argumentation.

16. God is objective in his Oneness and subjective in his Threeness (personhood).

CHAPTER THREE

1. Acts 17:28

2. 1 John 4:19

3. Matthew 28:19; 2 Corinthians 13:13; Didache 7:1-3.

4. This language might be confusing since Jesus is referred to as the "only begotten Son" in John 3:16. However, this verse is speaking specifically about the human nature of Jesus. The reason for this statement is to assure the reader that there has been no other that God has incarnated upon the Earth—Jesus is the only begotten.

5. Oden, Thomas C. *Classic Christianity.* New York: Harper Collins, 1992, 54.

6. Matthew 26:36–46.

7. This was a Christological heretical movement in the Early Church which is attributed to Arius (c. AD 256–336), a Christian presbyter in Alexandria, Egypt.

8. This is particularly argued by Wayne Grudem, who is a theologian and co-founder of the Council on Biblical Manhood and Womanhood.

9. Matthew 26:36-46, as one example.

10. John 6:38.

11. This is my re-articulation of the classical logical "problem of evil" argument. I believe the classical rendering of this argument is problematic and that this is a better way to articulate the problem while maintaining the logical intent.

12. An idea borrowed from Gottfried Leibniz.

13. Side note for the sake of philosophical clarity. Plantinga was not Leibnizian. My re-articulation of the thinking produced by all three philosophers is my own and is meant to show how each, in their own thinking, can coalesce into a hybrid argument. Likewise, Leibniz was not Augustinian. I agree with Plantinga - that Leibniz's second premise is problematic - but only in how he chose to defend it. I still agree with Leibniz's conclusion even though his second premise wasn't defended well. I don't

believe that it is necessary to say that just because God is good, it necessitates that he must also select the greatest possible world and that those within that world (or even the events that take place) are, in and of themselves, the best possible good. Their greatest possible goodness is relative to whatever makes this world the greatest possible world, which includes free will. It is free will that is missing from Leibniz's argument. This was Plantinga's perspective as well. This is why it is necessary to include all three individuals in this re-articulation.

14. See the section on prayer in Chapter 6 of this book for more of this discussion.

15. Colossians 1:16; John 1:3.

CHAPTER FOUR

1. Horsley, Richard A. "Popular Messianic Movements around the Time of Jesus." In *The Catholic Biblical*. Vol. 46, No. 3 (July, 1984), pp. 471-495.

https://www.jstor.org/stable/43716732.

2. John 14:6-7.

3. Primarily Penal Substitution Theory, but there are varying atonement views within evangelicalism.

4. John 1:1.

5. Philippians 2:6-7.

6. Luke 10:27.

7. John 6:38; John 5:19.

8. Schaff, Peter, and Wace, Henry. *Nicene and Post-Nicene Fathers, First Series, Vol. 3. On Faith And The Creed*. Buffalo: Christian Literature Publishing Co., 1892,325.

9. John 4:27.

10. Luke 8:1-3.

11. Luke 13:16.

12. Luke 4:16-30; Pelikan, Jaroslav. *The Illustrated Jesus Through the Centuries*. New Haven: Yale University Press, 1997, 9-23.

13. Matthew 3:13-17.

14. Matthew 16:13-20.

15. Helen Rhee, Early Christian Literature, (London: Routledge, 2005), 159–161.

16. Urs Von Balthasar, Hans. *A Theology of History*. San Francisco: Ignatius Press, 1994, 29-30.

17. Luke 23:3.

18. See Chapter 2 for more about this.

19. 2 Corinthians 5:21.

20. The reason for using the English Standard Version (ESV) in this case as opposed to the New International Version (NIV) (which the majority of this book uses) is because the NIV translates the passage incorrectly. The NIV relies on dynamic equivalence, meaning it is up to the translator (and reviewers) to decide how to render the text. I used the ESV not for proof-texting reasons, but because it is based upon a more literal translation and rendered the Hebrew correctly. In fact, all literal translations render this passage this way. Since proper translation is important for this section, I made the choice to stay with the ESV for the remainder of this section to ensure that the translation was accurate.

21. 1 Corinthians 15:22-45.

22. Giles, Keith. *Jesus Unforsaken: Substituting Divine Wrath with Unrelenting Love*. Quoir, March 23, 2021, 86.

23. Ibid., 178.

24. 1 Corinthians 15:45-49.

25. Matthew 24:36.

26. 1 Corinthians 15:52.

27. John 3:16.

28. John 14:12.

29. Romans 11:11-24

CHAPTER FIVE

1. Cole. Graham. *He Who Gives Life: The Doctrine of the Holy Spirit, Foundations of Evangelical Theology Series*. Ed. John S. Feinberg. Crossway: 2007.

2. 1 Kings 8:10-12.

3. 1 Corinthians 6:19.

4. The "father," "son" and "Holy Spirit" formula has also been used in early baptismal creeds and other early church documents.

5. John 14:15-18.

6. John 14:16, 26.

7. Romans 8:26.

8. 1 Corinthians 14.

9. Irenaeus, *The Ante-Nicene Fathers, In Ten Volumes, Book III*. Ed. Alexander Roberts – James Donaldson. New York: Charles Scribner's Sons, 1885), 531.

10. Tertullian, *The Ante-Nicene Fathers, In Ten Volumes, Book III*. Ed. Alexander Roberts – James Donaldson. New York: Charles Scribner's Sons, 1885), 445-447.

11. The philosopher Celsus, in the 2nd century, also claimed that Christians were speaking in tongues.

12. May, L. Carlyle. "A Survey of Glossolalia and Related Phenomena in Non-Christian Religions,." *American Anthropologist*, 58, No. 1, February 1956, 58.

13. 1 Corinthians 3:16.

14. 1 Corinthians 6:19.

15. 1 Corinthians 12:12-27.

16. John 14:15-18.

17. Romans 13:14.

18. A term popularized by Martin Heidegger that suggests a link that exists between existence and action within the world.

19. James 2:14-26.

20. John 14:13.

21. Matthew 17:20.

22. Or one could argue that the universe deemed the event to occur.

23. Romans 8:26.

24. 1 Thessalonians 5:16-18.

25. LeFevre, Perry D. *The prayers of Kierkegaard*. Chicago: University of Chicago Press, 1996, 9.

26. Mark 14:36.

CHAPTER SIX

1. Fackre, Gabriel. *The Christian Story: A Narrative Interpretation of Basic Christian Doctrine*. Grand Rapids, Eerdmans 1996, 63-64.

2. Literally, "five books."

3. Enns, Peter and Byas, Jared. *Genesis for Normal People: A Guide to the Most Controversial, Misun_

derstood, and Abused Book of the Bible. Independently Published.

4. Romans 1:20

5. Much of Genesis is mythological.

6. There is debate on the translation of Genesis 1. Different translations make different assumptions, and, in some cases, creation is not ex nihilo and in other cases it is. Since Hebrews 11:3 verifies creation ex nihilo I make the assumption that this is the case. I have not included this debate in the text as it is not important for the task at hand.

7. Matthew 19.

8. As found in the book by the same name. Ricoeur, Paul. *Oneself as Another*. Chicago: University of Chicago Press, 1990.

9. Ricoeur, Paul. *Time and Narrative*. Chicago: University of Chicago Press, 1983.

10. A term used by Thomas Aquinas to describe humanity's longing for sin over being obedient.

11. Genesis 3:23-24.

12. Genesis 3:7,16.

13. Genesis 3:16-18.

14. Fackre, Gabriel. *The Doctrine of Revelation: A Narrative Interpretation*. Grand Rapids: Wm. B. Eerdmans, 1997, 43-44.

15. John 6:38.

16. Romans 5:12–21.

17. An idea articulated by German theologian Dietrich Bonhoeffer that emphasizes the community as the people of God instead of the more formalized institution.

18. Luke 15:11-32.

CHAPTER SEVEN

1. Popularized by Paul Ricoeur in his book Oneself as Another.

2. Oden, Classic Christianity, 691.

3. Matthew 16:17-19.

4. Matthew 6:20.

5. Revelation 21:1-3.

6. As well as Matthew 5:26.

7. Bentley Hart, David Bentley. *Atheist Delusions: The Christian Revolution and Its Fashionable Ene_mies*. New Haven: Yale University Press, 2009.

8. 1 Timothy 2:4

9. I do not include the book of Revelation in this conversation due to its highly analogous nature. It is not clear if there is anything within the apocalyptic book that can be taken literally.

10. 1 Timothy 2:3-4 says nearly the same thing.

11. Wenig, Steffen. *Africa In Antiquity: The Essays*. Volume I. New York: The Brooklyn Museum, 1978, 98.

12. Fernea, Robert A. and Gerster, Georg. *Nubians in Egypt*. Austin: University of Texas Press, 1973, 121.

13. de Vallombreuse, Pierre and Savin, Tristan. *Souveraines: Ces peuples où les femmes sont libres*. Paris: Arthaud, 2015.

14. Aristotle. *Aristotle's Politics*. Oxford: Clarendon Press, 1905.

15. Aristotle, Cresswell, Richard and Gottlob Schneider, Johann. *Aristotle's History of Animals, In Ten Books*. London: H.G. Bohn, 1862.

16. Muddiman, John and Barton, John. *The Oxford Bible Commentary*. New York: Oxford University Press, 2001, 1130.

17. Romans 1:1-16.

18. Romans 16.

19. Adoption and Foster Care Analysis and Reporting System (AFCARS), FY 2020, U.S. Department of Health and Human Services, Administration for Children and Families, Children's Bureau. November 30, 2021.

https://www.acf.hhs.gov/cb/report/trends-foster-care-adoption. Submissions as of October 4, 2021.

20. Barna Research Group, "5 Things You Need To Know About Adoption." *Barna*. November 4, 2013.

https://www.barna.com/research/5-things-you-need-to-know-about-adoption/#.UnvPco2E7Tw.
Note:
This same study showed that "practicing Christians" are more than twice as likely to adopt than the general population.

21. Pew Research Center, "Key Findings about U.S. Immigrants." July 10, 2021.

https://www.pewresearch.org/fact-tank/2020/08/20/key-findings-about-u-s-immigrants/.

22. Guttmacher Institute, "Characteristics of U.S. Abortion Patients in 2014 and Changes Since 2008," July 10, 2021.

https://www.guttmacher.org/report/characteristics-us-abortion-patients-2014.

23. Children's Defense Fund, "The State of America's Children 2020 - Child Poverty," July 10, 2021.

https://www.childrensdefense.org/policy/resources/soac-2020-child-poverty/.

24. American Institutes for Research, "National Center on Family Homelessness," July 10, 2021.

https://www.air.org/project/national-center-family-homelessness.

25. Guttmacher, "Characteristics of U.S. Abortion Patients."

26. Kobes Du Mez, Kristin. *Jesus and John Wayne: How White Evangelicals Corrupted a Faith and Fractured a Nation*. New York, NY: Liveright, 2020, 169.

27. Ibid.,170-172.

28. I am only focusing on homosexuality for simplicity's sake, but some of the same arguments can be applied to other forms of sexuality as well.

29. McCarthy, Justin. "Same-Sex Marriage Support Inches Up to A New High of 71%." *Gallup*. June 1, 2022.

https://news.gallup.com/poll/393197/same-sex-marriage-support-inches-new-high.aspx.

30. The Trevor Project, "Facts About LGBT Youth Suicide", accessed July 31, 2022.

https://www.thetrevorproject.org/resources/article/facts-about-lgbtq-youth-suicide/.

31. Green, Amy E., Price, Myeshia N., and Dorison, Sam H. "Cumulative minority stress and suicide risk among LGBTQ youth." *The American Journal of Community Psychology*, Vol 69, Issue 1-2, March 2022, 157-168.

32. It is most common in today to refer to "homosexuals" as being "gay" or in "same-sex" relationships. (I acknowledge the language has evolved beyond this, but I will adhere to this social convention for efficiency in hopes that it does not offend anyone with its simplicity.) However, I refer to those in biblical times as "homosexuals" or "bisexuals" more specifically in order to distinguish between those who practiced such acts recreationally versus those who desire to be in committed same-sex relationships.

33. Ferrari, Gloria. *Figures of Speech: Men and Maidens in Ancient Greece*. Chicago: University of Chicago Press, 2002, 127; Dodd, D.B. "Athenian Ideas about Cretan Pederasty," in Thomas K. Hubbard (ed.), *Greek Love Reconsidered*. New York: 2000, 33-41; Ephorus of Cyme, "Fragment 149″, found in Thomas K. Hubbard. Berkeley: University of California Press, 2003, 72-73.

34. McClure, Laura. *Sexuality and gender in the classical world: readings and sources. Interpreting ancient history*. Oxford: Blackwell Publishers, 2002.

35. Vines, Matthew. *God and the Gay Christian: The Biblical Case in Support of Same-Sex Relationships*. New York: Convergent Books, 2014, 103-104.

36. Ibid.,108-110.

37. Ibid.,108.

38. This, of course, is based on a premise that homosexual behavior is sin to begin with. I leave the answer to that question up to the reader.

39. Vandermaas-Peeler, Alex, Cox, Daniel, et. al. "Partisan Polarization Dominates Trump Era: Find ings from the 2018 American Values Survey." *PRRI*. Oct. 29, 2018. https://www.prri.org/research/partisan-polarization-dominates-trump-era-find ings-from-the-2018-american-values-survey/.

40. Martin Heidegger, Being and Time, Translated by John MacQuarrie & Edward Robinson. (Lon don: SCM Press, 1962).

41. 1 John 4:6.

CHAPTER EIGHT

1. Philippians 2:12.

APPENDIX A

1. Perhaps more like the Letter to the Romans.

BIBLIOGRAPHY

Aristotle. *Aristotle's Politics.* Oxford: Clarendon Press, 1905.

Aristotle, Richard Cresswell, and Johann Gottlob Schneider. *Aristotle's History of Animals, In Ten Books.* London: H.G. Bohn, 1862.

Borg, Marcus J. *Reading the Bible Again for the First Time: Taking the Bible Seriously but not Literally.* San Francisco, CA: HarperCollins, 2002.

Cole, Graham. *He Who Gives Life: The Doctrine of the Holy Spirit, Foundations of Evangelical Theology Series, ed. John S. Feinberg.* Wheaton: Crossway, 2007.

D. B. Dodd, "Athenian Ideas about Cretan Pederasty," in Thomas K. Hubbard (ed.), *Greek Love Reconsidered*, New York: 2000, 33-41.

de Vallombreuse, Pierre and Tristan Savin. Souveraines: Ces peuples où les femmes sont libres. Paris: Arthaud, 2015.

Du Mez, Kristin Kobes. *Jesus and John Wayne: How White Evangelicals Corrupted a Faith and Fractured a Nation.* New York, NY: Liveright, 2020.

Enns, Peter and Jared Byas. *Genesis for Normal People: A Guide to the Most Controversial, Misunderstood, and Abused Book of the Bible.* Englewood, CO: Patheos Press, 2012.

Ephorus of Cyme, "Fragment 149", found in Thomas K. Hubbard, Berkeley: University of California Press, 2003, 72-73.

Fackre, Gabriel. *The Christian Story: A Narrative Interpretation of Basic Christian Doctrine.* Grand Rapids: Eerdmans, 1996.

Fackre, Gabriel. *The Doctrine of Revelation: A Narrative Interpretation.* Grand Rapids: Eerdmans, 1997.

Fernea, Robert A and Georg Gerster. *Nubians in Egypt.* Austin: University of Texas Press, 1973.

Ferrari, Gloria. *Figures of Speech: Men and Maidens in Ancient Greece,* Chicago: University of Chicago Press, 2002, 127.

Giles, Keith. *Jesus Unforsaken: Substituting Divine Wrath With Unrelenting Love.* Quoir, 2021.

Green, Amy E., Myeshia N. Price, and Sam H. Dorison. "Cumulative minority stress and suicide risk among LGBTQ youth." *The American Journal of Community Psychology.* 69, Issue 1-2. (March 2022): 157-168.

Grudem, Wayne A. *Systematic Theology: an Introduction to Biblical Doctrine.* Leicester: Inter-Varsity Press, 1994.

Hart, David Bentley. *Atheist Delusions: The Christian Revolution and Its Fashionable Enemies.* New Haven: Yale University Press, 2009.

Heidegger, Martin. *Being and Time,* Translated by John MacQuarrie & Edward Robinson. London: SCM Press, 1962.

Horsley, Richard A., "Popular Messianic Movements around the Time of Jesus," *The Catholic Biblical* 46, no. 3 (July, 1984): 471-495.

Irenaeus. *The Ante-Nicene Fathers, In Ten Volumes.* New York: Charles Scribner's Sons, 1918.

Jones, Jeffrey, "U.S. Church Membership Falls Below Majority for First Time," *Gallup*, March 29, 2021,

Jones, Tony. *The New Christians, Dispatches From the Emergent Frontier.* San Francisco, CA: Jossey-Bass, 2008.

Kierkegaard, Soren. *The Purity of Heart is to Will One Thing.* New York, NY: Harper Torchbooks, 1956.

Kierkegaard, Soren. *Practice in Christianity.* Princeton, NJ.: Princeton University Press, 1991.

LeFevre, Perry D. *The Prayers of Kierkegaard*. Chicago: University of Chicago Press, 1996.

Lindbeck, George. *The Nature of Doctrine: Religion and Theology in a Postliberal Age*. London, Westminster: John Knox Press, 1984.

May, L. Carlyle, "A Survey of Glossolalia and Related Phenomena in Non-Christian Religions," *American Anthropologist* 58, no. 1 (February 1956): 75-96.

McCarthy, Justin, "Record-High 70% in U.S. Support Same-Sex Marriage," *Gallup* (June 8, 2021). https://news.gallup.com/poll/350486/record-high-support-same-sex-marriage.aspx.

McLaren, Brian. *Faith After Doubt: Why Your Beliefs Stopped Working and What To Do About It*. New York: St. Martin's Essentials, 2021.

McClure, Laura. *Sexuality and gender in the classical world: readings and sources. Interpreting ancient history*. Oxford, UK/Malden, MA: Blackwell Publishers, 2002.

Muddiman, John and John Barton. *The Oxford Bible Commentary*. New York: Oxford University Press Inc., 2001.

Oden, Thomas C. *Classic Christianity*. New York, NY: Harper Collins, 1992.

Pelikan, Jaroslav. *The Illustrated Jesus Through the Centuries*. New Haven: Yale University Press, 1997.

Rhee, Helen. *Early Christian Literature*. London: Routledge, 2005.

Ricoeur, Paul. *Oneself as Another*. Chicago: University of Chicago Press, 1990.

Ricoeur, Paul. *Time and Narrative*. Chicago: University of Chicago Press, 1983.

Schaff, Philip and Henry Wace. *Nicene and Post-Nicene Fathers, First Series, Vol. 3*. Buffalo, NY: Christian Literature Publishing Co., 1892.

Schaff, Philip and Henry Wace. *Nicene and Post-Nicene Fathers, Second Series, Vol. 4*. Buffalo, NY: Christian Literature Publishing Co., 1892.

Tertullian, *The Ante-Nicene Fathers, In Ten Volumes*. New York: Charles Scribner's Sons, 1918.

Vandermaas-Peeler, Alex, Daniel Cox, Maxine Najle, Ph. D., Molly Fisch-Friedman, Rob Griffin, Ph. D., and Robert P. Jones, Ph. D., "Partisan Polarization Dominates Trump Era: Findings from the 2018 American Values Survey," PRII, October 29, 2018,

Vines, Matthew. *God and the Gay Christian: The Biblical Case in Support of Same-Sex Relationships*. New York: Convergent Books, 2014.

Von, Balthasar Hans Urs. *A Theology of History*. San Francisco: Ignatius Press, 1994.

Wenig, S. *Africa In Antiquity: The Essays, Volume I*. New York: The Brooklyn Museum, 1978: 98.

Whyte, W. H. Jr. "Groupthink." *Fortune,* (March 1952): 114-117, 142, 146.

For more information about Eric Scot English,
or to contact him for speaking engagements,
please visit www.ericsenglish.com.

For more resources related to this book,
please visit UnenlightenmentTheBook.com.

Many Voices. One Message.

Quoir is a boutique publisher
with a singular message: *Christ is all*.
Venture beyond your boundaries to discover Christ
in ways you never thought possible.

For more information, please visit
www.quoir.com

www.ingramcontent.com/pod-product-compliance
Lightning Source LLC
Chambersburg PA
CBHW071322120626
46546CB00002B/395